God's Guinea Pig

Barbara.

With every blessing.

Margaret Heuman

High Leigh.
On fire 2004

GORDON and BARBARA WALLACE
33 Park Lane
Hornchurch
Essex
RM11 1BD
Tel: 01708 720841

God's Guinea Pig

Margaret Freeman

iUniverse, Inc.
New York Lincoln Shanghai

God's Guinea Pig

All Rights Reserved © 2004 by Margaret Freeman

No part of this book may be reproduced or transmitted in any form or by any means, graphic, electronic, or mechanical, including photocopying, recording, taping, or by any information storage retrieval system, without the written permission of the publisher.

iUniverse, Inc.

For information address:
iUniverse, Inc.
2021 Pine Lake Road, Suite 100
Lincoln, NE 68512
www.iuniverse.com

ISBN: 0-595-31056-7

Printed in the United States of America

For Peter

Contents

Chapter 1	BEGINNINGS	1
Chapter 2	THE GUINEA PIG FACES DEATH	5
Chapter 3	THE GUINEA PIG GOES TO SCHOOL	10
Chapter 4	WAR	14
Chapter 5	EXAMS	21
Chapter 6	THE GUINEA PIG GOES TO COLLEGE	27
Chapter 7	DEATH AND RESURRECTION	35
Chapter 8	THE GUINEA PIG LIVES AGAIN	42
Chapter 9	PARISH LIFE	47
Chapter 10	CANADA	53
Chapter 11	LOVE AND MARRIAGE	59
Chapter 12	THE GUINEA-PIG MAKES HISTORY	65
Chapter 13	MARGARET CLARE	69
Chapter 14	TRAGEDY	73
Chapter 15	THE FAMILY GROWS	77
Chapter 16	HOTEL LIFE	81
Chapter 17	SURPRISE, SURPRISE—MARTIN CHARLES	84
Chapter 18	PASTURES NEW	89

Chapter 19	NOTHING LASTS FOREVER	93
Chapter 20	MY ANNUS HORIBILIS	98
Chapter 21	MUMMY DIES	103
Chapter 22	THE GUINEA PIG SURVIVES AGAIN	106
Chapter 23	GREAT YARMOUTH, HERE WE COME	112
Chapter 24	LIFE GIRLS	116
Chapter 25	THE GUINEA PIG IS BLESSED BY THE HOLY SPIRIT	121
Chapter 26	DOGS	127
Chapter 27	NEW CHALLENGES	134
Chapter 28	MAKING ENDS MEET	137
Chapter 29	TO BE OR NOT TO BE	139
Chapter 30	MANY GUINEA PIGS	144
EPILOGUE		149
About the Author		151

Acknowledgements

I wish to thank all those who for a long time have helped and encouraged me in the writing of this book. To Martin, who took copies off my old word processor and taught me to use a computer; to Shelly, who read the earlier chapters and encouraged me to continue; to all the other members of my family, without whom this book could not have been written; to the late Lord Brock and all my other doctors who have kept me alive, and all my colleagues in the Church who have supported and prayed for me. Thank you to Bill Bracey who proofread and made sense out of my efforts; thank you to the person who rang one evening and gave me Charles Muller's address without giving a name. It may have been an angel as I have never discovered the person's identity; and thank you, Charles and Diadem Books, for your encouragement. Most of all, I want to thank my dearest Peter to whom this book is dedicated. We became one on February 23rd 1957. Half of us went to God on July 24th 1975 while the other half is trying to finish our pilgrimage here on earth. I have been conscious throughout the writing of *God's Guinea Pig* that he has been writing it with me.

Margaret Freeman

1

BEGINNINGS

On a hot June afternoon in 1927 in the summer that women were granted the vote, and after a long and painful childbirth for her mother, the Guinea Pig arrived and was laid on her back in a cot where she proceeded to scream.

My mother believed strongly that character was formed from the moment of birth and that no child should be picked up because of screaming. When she could stand the cries no longer she discovered that if I was propped on a pillow or turned on my side, I was quiet and slept. I was eighteen months old when they discovered that my screaming was nature's way of enabling me to get enough air in my lungs to breathe. My mother never forgave herself for being so harsh with me. She told me on many occasions that her first words on seeing me were, "What terrible hands!" My mother was one who always noticed people's hands (something which I have inherited from her) and when she hoped to see tiny, dainty, baby hands on her precious firstborn, she saw fat, podgy mitts with short fingers and big bulbous fingertips. The short fingers I inherited from my father, but the big bulbous blue ends with wide nails are a hallmark of the condition that was later to be diagnosed.

My sister arrived sixteen months later, and like me, was born at home and delivered by the family doctor. She was a model baby. After her birth I developed a cold and, mother being anxious that I should not infect the new baby, she asked the doctor to have a look at me. My mother was also by now a little concerned that I made no effort to walk or crawl, preferring to sit and shuffle on my bottom for movement. Unbelievable as it seems today, it was not until then that a stethoscope was put on me for the first time in my life and the doctor heard my strange heart noises. My mother was instructed to take me to the surgery for a full investigation as soon as she had recovered from her confinement.

"I am sorry, Mrs Adams, but your daughter has a very serious congenital heart defect. If you take great care of her she will probably live until she is about seven. She will be very small and her arms and legs will be very thin. She will never walk unaided and will spend a lot of time squatting on her haunches, because this helps her breathing." My mother heard the news and stoically took me home and got on with the business of raising her two small daughters. I think she must have believed in miracles because, while taking extra care of me and watching over me carefully, she allowed me to develop at my own pace.

My parents had, from the time of their marriage, lived in a flat at the top of my grandmother's Clapham house. With two small children to lug upstairs, this was impractical, so they bought a bungalow in Great Missenden. We only lived there a couple of years and my memories of it revolve around two events—sitting watching my parents pick apples in the Orchard, and my second birthday present. The night before this momentous day I woke to hear my parents' voices outside our bedroom door. The door opened and a small wriggly bundle was put on my bed, and it proceeded to lick my face and run over the blanket. It was a small black Cocker Spaniel! I named him Billy and we were inseparable. I crawled around the floor with him and shared his basket. Sadly, at the age of two, he was to escape and disappear on Guy Fawke's night, probably frightened by the noise. For weeks we searched, and many visits to Battersea dogs' home were made with no success. It was to be the start of a disastrous time with black Cockers, and was to give me a hatred of fireworks, which has remained with me all my life. I think my family was jinxed dog-wise at that time. Bess arrived, this time a present for my sister Sheila. We had her eight days when the vet pronounced that she had perforated insides and she was put to sleep. As I had on her first day crawled into the kitchen and picked her up only to have her squirm out of my arms, I suffered agonies of childish guilt, which I never shared with anyone. I was a murderer of dogs and cried myself to sleep for weeks. As I couldn't possibly have lifted her more than a couple of feet, I am pretty sure now I was in no way responsible. Bess was soon followed by Bill the second, a big, butch, healthy specimen. In those days there was no immunisation against distemper and the majority of dogs who caught it either died or had to be destroyed. Sadly Bill was to catch it while we were on our annual holiday and, despite all the efforts of my mother and the vet, just as he seemed to be making progress, the dreaded virus attacked his brain. After days of watching the poor creature walk round in circles, even my mother had to admit defeat and he was put out of his misery. It was many years before we had another dog.

After two years at South Missenden my mother was pregnant again. My father was fed up with having to leave home at seven o'clock each morning to get to work at the Bank of England and, because their relationship was never very secure due to his wandering eye, my mother wanted to return to be near her mother and sisters. The top flat which had been our first home was let, but the house next door to my grandmother was available so my parents bought it and paid the mortgage by letting the top flat and a bed-sitting room on the middle landing.

We all stayed with Grannie for my mother's confinement and well I remember the night Colin was born. I was nearly four and lay in my grandmother's big double bed where my mother had slept from the night my grandfather died until her wedding day. My sister was asleep in her cot by my side. I longed for Grannie to come to bed, but she never came and in the early hours of the morning my father came and carried me in to see my baby brother.

Colin seemed to me the most perfect creature in the world. When I was allowed to sit back in a big chair and hold him, my cup of joy knew no bounds. As a four-year old I wanted to share in all his care, and a bond developed between us, which was to remain with me after his death ten weeks later. The doctor said to have two children with congenital heart defects was very unusual and my mother should have no more children. In those days there was very little means of regulating one's family, and my father who already found fidelity difficult had now good reason to seek his carnal satisfaction elsewhere. That is not to say he did not love my mother. He was devoted to her and would have given her the earth. He was also very good to my widowed grandmother, for whom he had great respect and called Mrs Barton which seems strange nowadays; this in spite of the fact we all lived so closely together. He managed her affairs until her dying day and they were in fact extremely fond of each other.

My father's parents lived at Clacton and, as he was an only child, my parents believed that every holiday should be spent visiting them. However, my mother never wished to associate with any other members of his family unless forced to do so. To understand the background of this one would have to understand the social differences, which were so strong in those days. My mother had been engaged to a gentleman of her own social class who, when he discovered my grandmother was a penniless widow, having lost her husband in the 1919 'flu epidemic, wanted her to go and make her home abroad. My grandmother's eldest daughter had already married well and gone to live in the USA, so my mother refused to go, broke off the engagement and started going around with a handsome young man in the Bank of England where she and her brother both worked. The match was unsuitable—a fact which families on both sides found difficult to cope with—but to my mother's eternal credit she did care for her parents-in-law and tried to be a daughter to them. When Colin was three weeks old and after his christening, another event made a great impact on my four-year old mind: I was packed off to Clacton to my paternal grandparents.

My grandmother, who had always suffered from not being able to produce a daughter, dressed me like a doll, curled my hair in ringlets and pushed me round in my wheelchair to show me off to all her neighbours. She spoilt me, played with me, read to me, and I would probably have enjoyed it had I not been so aware of what was going on at home. To imagine that any four-year old can be shut out from family tension is ridiculous, and because of my limited physical capabilities, I believe I was more aware than most. I knew Colin was very ill, I knew my mother was very unhappy, longed to be near her to comfort her, and I was jealous of my sister who was not sent away as it was believed she was too young to be affected by the situation. Also, Colin was dying of serious heart deformity, and although not so bad, I also had very limited life expectancy. Maybe my parents were right to do as they did, but it is not something I would do for any of my children. I am truly glad that with the wonderful hospices for sick children which we now have in many parts of the country the emphasis is on keeping the whole family together, whilst recognising each member's needs. I am sure this is right. I am told I was being so difficult that in the end I was allowed home. When my mother saw her elder daughter looking like a character from a Jane Austen novel she was not too pleased and a certain coolness existed between her and her mother-in-law for quite a while.

Colin's last few days were spent in hospital. Mother had brought him back from the dead with whisky on several occasions, as this seemed to stimulate his deformed heart, but it was a hopeless task. He died gasping for breath and my father and the hospital refused to let her see him. She never got over this and blamed my father for the rest of her life. I believe that because she was never allowed to hold her child and grieve, as she would be able to nowadays, she became rather hard and unforgiving. Also, she had to live with the fact that my life expectancy was extremely short, and with my father's unfaithfulness, life for her was a lot tougher than I realised for many years.

2

THE GUINEA PIG FACES DEATH

Around the time of Colin's death my parents took on what was commonly known in those days as a 'mother's help.' This was an Irish girl, a vegetarian with a simple Roman Catholic faith. At first I resented her and played her up, refusing to let her do anything for me. I believe I was still suffering from being sent away when Colin was ill and was very demanding of my mother's attention, which must have added considerably to the strain she was under. Clare (or Nanny, as we called her) was very good with Sheila, and for a long time she looked after her, giving my mother more time for me. However, I was afraid of broaching the subject of Colin's death to mother for fear of upsetting her. To me he was still very real and somehow passed into my imagination. Whereas other children had imaginary friends to talk to them in their loneliness, I had Colin. I talked to him endlessly, a fact which did not go unnoticed by Nanny. One day she took the opportunity of mentioning Colin to me. My relief knew no bounds, and for hours we talked incessantly about him, about his death, about the hereafter, and about the fact that he was with me as my guardian angel. She gave me a book *Wapsy: the Story of a Guardian Angel*, which she read to me and I very soon learned to read for myself. It had wonderful pictures and was my most treasured possession. She suggested that I pray for Colin who was in a beautiful garden where, because he was so young and sinless when he died, he most assuredly was. She also suggested to me that as I had been so disagreeable towards her, I needed to pray for forgiveness if I was ever to join Colin in Jesus' Garden. This I did unreservedly. Best of all, she suggested that I ask Colin to pray for me always. The thought of never seeing Colin again was more than I could bear, and I am still conscious of his prayers and support. I also prayed fervently that my mother would give me another brother, but she never did.

Partly, I believe, for the sake of their marriage, and partly because they believed it was good for us, my parents went out about once a week, leaving us with Grannie next door and our two young aunts. This meant we did not sleep in our own beds but in the spare room in Grannie's house, the room in which Colin had been born. I detested this, being quite sure that if I fell asleep in a bed other than my own I would never wake again. I was four! Five! Six! Memories of the doctor's words that if my mother looked after me I would live to Seven! Part of me wanted to see Colin, but would I ever be good enough to go to that 'Garden'! Another part of me feared leaving those I loved. Life was not all that bad. As I lay in the bed next door, Sheila slumbering childishly and peacefully, it seemed often that sleep would never come. My young Aunt Vida seemed, more than anyone, to understand my fears, and when others scolded me for not "cuddling down and going to sleep," would creep up and stand just inside the door after promising me that she would not leave me until I was finally asleep. I am grateful to this day for her great understanding.

In the spring before my seventh birthday I caught 'flu. Then quite suddenly one day my nose started to bleed, but not a little bleed. It poured and nothing anyone could do would make it stop. It was obvious that my racing heart was not going to keep up with the necessity of making new blood and I was slowly bleeding to death. The doctor came and stuffed my nose in a desperate effort to stop me losing any more blood. I slept, or rather lay in a semi-coma between my mother and grandmother who held tightly all night to my hands to prevent me pulling out the plugging. In the morning I was better and the doctor removed the plug. However, because of the uncertainty of what was going to happen next, he sent me to hospital. As everyone seemed convinced this was the end they had all been waiting for, I was put into an adult ward; it would have been too upsetting for the other children to have me die in the children's ward. I had been there only a few hours when a lady was pushed in on a trolley. She was deathly pale and was immediately surrounded by a number of doctors and nurses, who all stood around with gloomy faces. Whenever she was left alone she moaned, and they rushed back. I lay watching, afraid to ask what was going on, but sure in my childish mind that this was another encounter with death. Is this what Colin had looked like? Soon my parents came and I asked what was going on opposite me. Realising my distress I think my father must have said something to the nurse, as very soon screens were put across the end of the bed and I never saw the woman again, although the noise continued all night. In the morning the curtains were pulled back and she had gone. I prayed for her—and for me!

Because of the seriousness of my condition, I was allowed visitors at any time. My parents would come around lunch time and sit by me until I went to sleep, returning in the evening to give me my supper, which was always bread and cheese and cocoa served to the whole ward from a big white enamel jug. Afterwards they would stay with me until I settled for the night. On about the third day, possibly because I was a little better, I cried. A junior nurse spotted my tears and rushed to tell the staff nurse who bent over me, her face a few inches from mine, and told me that if I didn't stop instantly she would not allow my parents in that night. A few minutes later, I saw her talking to them in the doorway. I lay, hardly daring to breathe, let alone cry, and heard raised voices until they were finally let in. I hated that staff nurse and the junior who had reported me and quaked whenever they came up the ward, but, with hindsight, I think she may have been very frightened that if I got too distressed my heart might give out under the strain while she was in charge. I have long ago forgiven her, but this would never be tolerated today. There was no National Health and this was a public ward and the amenities were of the most basic kind. Everyone, even the doctors, lived in fear of the ward sister who had enormous power. Doctors had to ask her permission to enter the ward, however sick the patient, junior nurses scuttling about, fearing to talk to the patients and woe betide even a very young patient if she dared to let her bed get untidy! "Ward tidies" were done every four hours when every possession was stuffed away in the locker with no thought of whether the item was accessible to the sick patient. As I was not allowed to move more than was absolutely necessary, I was bored stiff. Oh, the joy when I was allowed to sit out of bed one day and do a jigsaw brought me by my favourite aunt!

God fooled the lot of them and preserved the life of His guinea pig and I was allowed home to spend most of my time in bed and to see how things went. We went on our annual holiday to Clacton where my grandmother hired a long iron bed from the hospital on which I could lie in the garden and watch Sheila play. Gradually I got stronger and the family had to give in to my protests that I wanted to get around. My parents bought me a full-sized wheelchair and some very comfortable fitted cushions that I have to this day and use on a window seat. My mother also made me a big bag, which today would be called an outsize 'cosy toes.' It was very important that I was kept warm and now I could go out in the coldest weather without getting cold, although I was always nagged to keep a scarf over my mouth and never breathe cold air. Strangely enough I never felt the cold in those days, not nearly as much as I did when I learnt to walk. I developed a great love of sport and loved to be out of doors watching other kids playing football or rounders on Clapham common. My greatest treat was when my father pushed me to the common on a Saturday afternoon to watch the local football matches. He explained to me the finer points of the game and lots of people who came week after week would talk to the little girl in the wheelchair. As a result of this I developed a strong relationship with my father. He seemed proud of me despite my blue face and deformed hands and body, and, unlike most people, he happily accepted my peculiarities, teaching me to laugh at myself and to be open and honest about myself. Sometimes at bedtime he would come to say goodnight to us and pretend to stagger across the room, finally falling down breathing wheezily in the way I did when I made feeble attempts to walk. When we were all three hysterical with laughter my mother would come in and rebuke him fiercely, but I am sure to this day that this enabled both Sheila and me to have a much healthier attitude to my disability than we might otherwise have had.

I think that if I had not been handicapped I would have been an enthusiastic sportswoman. My mother was a very keen tennis player and once played lacrosse for the Putney Ladies team. One of my sons is a fitness and sports freak and both boys run in marathons, so it must run in the family. On Saturday mornings in the summer my mother played tennis with the local team. Being a very good player, she was much in demand for matches. Daddy was not a very good player and in any case I think mummy found him an embarrassment. She soon found herself a suitable partner and left us in Daddy's care, which we loved. He played school with us and taught us many things and then took us for walks on the common. We loved Saturdays.

Sheila had reached school age about the time I had recovered from my sojourn in hospital and it was deemed worth educating me. The help of a Miss Theresa Soper was sought and a long yellow wooden table purchased and the dining room was turned into a schoolroom. The daughter of a doctor friend of my parents with whom they played bridge once a week joined us. Jean was a delicate and rather spoilt child and had a rocking horse, which everyone except me was allowed to ride. The daughter of some bank friends also joined us and the daughter of the local dentist became the youngest member of the party. We were taught well and I think all enjoyed our lessons, but we were preserved from the rough and tumble of ordinary school life. The younger Miss Grace Soper came once a week to teach us music and painting. Thus we were taught until we moved house and the yellow table was replaced by a dining snooker table.

In 1935 my mother came in very early in the morning to tell us the King was dead. I did not know he was ill and was quite unperturbed, an emotion, or rather lack of it I found one was not expected to admit to. The day of the king's funeral was a busy one for Dad, as the day of the Jubilee two years previously had been. I must explain. Besides his work in the bank and his family, my father had two other very important strands in his life. He was a reserve Lieutenant Commander in the Royal Navy, which meant that he got an extra two weeks holiday a year to go on training with the Navy. He was also a special constable in the Metropolitan Police force. This meant that at any big events when extra police were needed, he donned uniform and with his truncheon in his pocket, would sally forth to line the streets or help with crowd control. We needed a spare room to keep all his uniforms in. I well remember the day I sat with my mother who had made herself a black dress, which, for some reason I do not understand, she had edged with green, while we listened to John Snagg describing the scene as the funeral cortege passed through the streets of London against the background of the Funeral March. This was before the days of television and it says something about the way events were made to live on radio that I, who was only eight at the time, could remember it.

I remember little of the reign of Edward VIII—only, towards the end of his reign, there was much whispering among the grown-ups, and then one evening when the whole family were at a show given by the children' dancing class that Sheila attended, the whole audience stayed behind to listen to the abdication speech on a portable wireless plugged into the footlights on the stage. We then all sang "God save the King" to the new King George.

Because he was roughly the same age as my father and the Queen the age of my mother and the two princesses very close in age to Sheila and me, it was hardly surprising that it was these "royals" who interested us most. We were fascinated by a book on the royal dogs and green with envy at the little house which the Duke of York (as he was then) had built for his daughters in Windsor Great Park. Little did we guess then that "Lilibet" as the nation knew her was to be our queen for so many years. The first time I saw a Cavalier King Charles Spaniel and knew I wanted one was when one of this new rare breed was given to the animal loving Margaret Rose.

I longed for a dog, rather impractical as I was in a chair and could not exercise it. Our only pets were a rather wild rescued stray tabby cat aptly named Tiger and a goldfish. The fish disappeared from its bowl and a search revealed it lying in the coal shed still alive. My resourceful mother put it back in its bowl, rubbed off the coal dust, replaced the water and it survived. Tiger's second attempt was more successful. He was the only pet who was to move to our new house with us.

3

THE GUINEA PIG GOES TO SCHOOL

When I was nine we moved from Clapham to Brentwood in Essex. On the way home from one of our regular holidays to Clacton, my father did a detour and happened upon a large Georgian house going cheap. Further investigation revealed that it had four enormous reception rooms, one a drawing room, one a smaller lounge, one a dining room and the largest a Billiard room. There was also a huge kitchen, a butler's pantry and two rooms for servants' sitting rooms. This was the ground floor. Upstairs there were four large bedrooms, a nursery and various servants' bedrooms, as well as two or three bathrooms. It was in a shocking condition and needed a lot spending on it. It was going very cheap as no one would take on the responsibility at that time. There was much talk of war. Hitler had already invaded Austria and Czechoslovakia seemed next. Because both my parents and my uncle were respected in the Bank of England, getting the necessary loan was not difficult. One of my aunts had left home and my grandmother found the upkeep of such a big London house too much for just two of them. So it was decided that they should come with us and rent several of the rooms from my father, and this would help financially all round; should my Father have to go to war, the rest of us would all be together in what he considered would be a safe area.

Immediately across the road from the main entrance of our house was a very small private school with some twenty pupils run by two sisters, the Misses Elsie and Dorothy Crowe. Elsie taught the older children and Dorothy taught the younger ones and took singing for the whole school. These kindly souls were persuaded to take the Guinea Pig and her sister, and for a time all was well. I was pushed across the road each morning and at playtime was wrapped up and put in my wheelchair outside to watch the other kids play. I enjoyed my lessons and I believe the teaching must have been quite good and probably gave me a good foundation for what was to come. Sheila, however, did not settle and my parents were wise enough to begin to realise that she was suffering from being the Guinea Pig's younger sister. She needed to get away from me and be herself.

At last my cries to have a dog again were heard and on our next holiday to Clacton my paternal grandmother presented me with a Pekinese puppy, which we called Bess. She was ideal for us. Sheila walked her until her little legs grew tired, when she would ride happily on my lap cuddled in my blanket. She was very successful and lived sixteen years. She was also highly intelligent and was to save my mother's life twice in the war. I was also given a pair of budgerigars in a large cage. I bred these in the laundry room, a warm room where ironing was done on the bedroom storey of our big house. I bought more cages and was able to sell finger-tame babies to my friends. People were afraid of having dogs and cats because of the threat of war and were turning more and more to small cheap pets. We had a young ginger cat because Sheila went riding on Saturday mornings and the stable cat had kittens so, of course, she came home with one.

My parents soon realised that in buying "Woodlands", Primrose Hill, they had bitten off more than they could chew. It was necessary that the house and long garden be divided and the larger half be sold as soon as it was sufficiently done up to be a good purchase. This meant that my grandmother and Aunt Vida must move out. With war coming they had no desire to buy property and were able to rent a very nice house owned by our teachers, the Misses Crowe. This meant they were still near and we all saw each other every day. Mother and Vida started playing tennis again and not long after that Vida met the man who was to become my Uncle Desmond. Granny was delighted, but I think she also felt very insecure. Vida had shared her home from the time she left school until she was thirty, and now she was to go away and leave her.

Around the time of the Munich crisis I caught jaundice and was very ill again. Miss Crowe sent over work for me to do in bed so that I should not fall too behind in my education. Because of the severity of my illness I slept for months with my mother, and poor Dad was forced to sleep in my bed in the nursery, which could not have done much for their married life. I well remember lying in the big double bed listening to Neville Chamberlain promising that war had been averted. After Christmas I recovered enough to return to school and the family settled down to prepare for Vida's wedding. A month later Granny, who had suffered all her life from duodenal ulcers, was found by a neighbour unconscious in a pool of blood. An ulcer had burst and she was rushed to hospital, and only just recovered in time for the wedding in May. No way could she live on her own, so she returned to make her home with us.

Having looked into the jaws of death for the second time at the age of eleven, every fibre of my being wanted to be normal. When other people caught a cold they took an aspirin, stayed in the warm for a few days and recovered (remember, this was before the days of antibiotics). With me it was months in bed, sweating out fevers and daily visits from the doctor. Sheila was to be a bridesmaid, the one little bridesmaid with two grown-up ones. I was never asked. I felt rejected, despised Vida who I always thought understood me, and hated Mother for not making it all right. None thought I might feel out of it or took the trouble to say they were frightened it would be too much for me.

Sheila went off looking wonderful and quite stole the show. I was forced into a pink coat that clashed abominably with my blue face in the photographs, with my straight pigtails poking out of a straw hat onto my round shoulders. I tried to hide as much as I could. I remember it as a day when everyone else was very happy.

We went on holiday to Clacton that summer. My father, who was a Lieutenant Commander with the Royal Naval Reserve, was called up and war seemed imminent. On Friday, September 1st, Hitler invaded Poland. In preparation for war everyone had been issued with gas masks and was urged to practise using them. I found them very difficult to wear; breathing was difficult enough as it was, without taking every breath through a rubber filter. I persevered. We were also instructed to make sure our houses could be blacked out at night and on the Friday night the nation was put on trial blackout. This meant that the air-raid wardens would patrol the streets to make sure no lights were showing. As the whole family, including Vida and Des, were together in Clacton and my Father had to report to his ship the next day, we all went to Clacton bandstand for a last performance which was to be held by torchlight. During the performance the only light was on the stage and that was dimmed as far as possible. We listened to the old marches and dance music and twice during the evening there were periods of community singing, but no chorus sheets were allowed. We had to sing from memory. As this was a special evening we were given programmes when we entered, for it was still quite light then. Every programme was numbered and it was suggested we commit this number to memory, as it would be too dark to look at the programme at the end of the evening. The performance ended and the numbers read out. I had won first prize. I was helped to the platform to receive my prize—a lovely suitcase. I remember the evening for many reasons, but chiefly because out of the hundreds there I had won a prize!

Next morning Mum went to see Dad off and Vida and Desmond went home to their house in Shenfield, leaving us with our three grandparents. Sunday morning, Sept 3rd, we sat in the garage having our elevenses of milk and banana sandwiches as Chamberlain told us on the radio that we were at war.

4
WAR

With Dad gone to sea the six of us (three grandparents, Mother, Sheila and me) tried to settle down together. It soon became obvious that if we were to spend the war years at Clacton we had to make plans. Not surprisingly our education was the first consideration. First, Sheila was enlisted at a big girls' school the other end of town. The busses ran along the front or she could cycle. My education presented a greater problem. There was a convent, which ran a small school, and they were prepared to take me. After some deliberation and many lectures from Mother not to listen to "those Catholics" and always to remember I was C. of E., it was decided to send me there. Mother had held a driving licence from the days when there were no tests, but never drove. She now decided that she must buy a car and have a few lessons, which she courageously did. I know she hated every moment she spent behind the wheel and never drove again after the war. She regarded it as part of the necessity of war.

My paternal grandparents had lived in their bungalow for most of their married life and were very set in their ways. Grandpa suffered with his nerves and a breakdown had forced him to retire from his work as a silversmith before he was sixty. He was an avid gardener and purchased the whole of the plot next door and all was laid out to perfection. They even had a croquet lawn, which was much in use when family came. His summer routine was:

5.00am: Rise and work in the garden until 8.00.

8.00am: Take my grandmother a cup of tea.

When we were on holiday he would take tea to my parents and to us a cup of milk and two Garibaldi biscuits. It never changed! I still love Garibaldi biscuits!

He would then prepare breakfast, which was served in bed to Grandma at 8.30.

He would then eat his breakfast and read the paper. We were expected to be on parade then.

9.30am: he would change into his bowling green clothes and cycle along the front to the club. I remember him riding, first a penny-farthing and then a big fixed-wheel effort.

12.55: he would arrive home, wash his hands and expect everyone to be sitting down to lunch by 1.00pm on the dot. How well I remember those desperate scrambles from the beach to be home before Grandpa.

The rest of the day ran to a similar timetable and they were always in bed with the lights out by 9.30. The only difference made in the winter was that he started the day by making rugs when it was too dark to go in the garden. He made some wonderful mats for all the family and in those days the wool all had to be cut by hand. Redicut was unheard of.

Grandma was nearly as disciplined. Monday was washday and all had to be dried, ironed and aired by nightfall. Tuesday was shopping, Wednesday baking, Thursday silver cleaning, and there was a lot of it because of Grandpa's job, and Friday was for cleaning and polishing. The fact that I remember it to this day shows what a ritual it was.

The strain of living with this was very difficult and Mum decided to rent a flat near the Convent, which meant she would not have to get the car out every day and could push me to school.

I thrived at the Convent and I think my ten months there made an enormous difference to me. The nuns were angelic. They did not just sit me outside to watch the others playing, but taught me to catch balls from the wheelchair. They even put me in the umpire's chair at the sports field, to umpire the school tennis matches. If we misbehaved we were sat in front of a picture of the Sacred Heart (the well-known picture of Jesus with his heart exposed) and told to look at it and think how our behaviour was making God sad. I was never made allowances for, as had happened in the past, and the wheelchair was in front of the shrine of the Sacred Heart on many occasions. We started the day with prayer, prayed again when we came in from break, at the end of the morning and at the beginning and end of the afternoon. If anything was missing we all stopped and prayed to St. Anthony. The lost item always seemed to turn up. I made a great friend who was a cradle Catholic, and I do not think either of us believed that our faith did not work. Once a month, on a Friday morning, all the Catholic girls went in pairs to Exposition. For twenty minutes they had to kneel in prayer before the Blessed Sacrament exposed in a big monstrance. The monstrance was of bronze and was shaped like a sun. The Sacramental Wafer was put in the centre. I begged the nuns to let me go to Exposition with my friend. I was so keen that despite the fact I was a Protestant, they allowed me to go one Friday. A chair replaced the prayer desk and I was allowed to sit in Our Lord's Presence. I considered it a great honour. In that twenty minutes I gave my life to God and heard Him speak to me. I also desperately wanted to become a Catholic. I talked with my form mistress who gave me a copy of the Catholic Catechism, which I soon learnt by heart. Paddy, my friend, started to come every Sunday morning to push me to Mass and I screwed up courage to tell my Mother. Her reaction was to start taking us to Matins at the local church, so that I could not go to Mass, although she did let me go occasionally.

In fairness to my mother I think I should explain that she certainly was not without faith. As young children in London we were told about once a month on a Saturday night to be very quiet in the morning as Mummy was going to the 8 o'clock. As it was never connected with God or Church, I at first believed it was something she did with Daddy, and when one day I found a book on sex in her bottom drawer I searched hard to find a mention of the 8 o'clock. Later I discovered she had a very real faith about which she was embarrassed. It was never to be shared and she got very upset if the vicar or anyone else spoke to her. I think she felt safe at the 8 o'clock service until at one church they started giving the peace. It was years before she went again.

Just occasionally, we were taken to a Children's service when on holiday at Clacton. Before we went I was told firmly never to answer the Vicar's questions as these were for the Sunday School children. My Mother believed that Sunday Schools were for the working classes. Nice little girls were supposed to learn what religion they needed at home. From my experience, that was almost nil. I am still deeply grateful for those precious few months at the Convent.

Such happiness could not last in wartime. During the time I was at St. Clare's Convent, Hitler had taken Belgium, Holland, Norway and Finland and was slowly eating up France. There seemed no stopping him and nothing bar a miracle could stop him invading England. The whole of the South and East Coast was like a fortress and most adult conversation seemed to be about where along the coast he would attack. The Channel and the North Sea were alive with shipping.

Suddenly one night an aircraft was heard overhead which seemed to be in trouble. Many people, including Mother, went to their doors to look out. It circled low over the Grand Hotel next door before dropping a bomb two roads away from my school and finally crashing down in the North Sea. It was the one and only bomb to be dropped on England before the fall of France and the Battle of Britain. Three of the girls in my class were killed, the school and Convent were badly damaged, and we lost our windows. We were protected by the hotel from a lot of the blast, but I was in bed and a wardrobe fell across me which sheltered me from flying glass. We got out of it without a scratch, but considerably shaken.

The news from France was getting worse and worse. Everyone was fleeing from the coast. My grandparents wanted to stay where they were and face the consequences. Within three days we had taken them the goldfish, had the cat put to sleep, hidden the silver under the floorboards and packed ourselves, Bess, the dog, the budgerigar and a few bags of clothes, gas masks and identity cards into the little car and were on the road.

We decided to go first to Shenfield to Vida while we decided what to do next. Dad's ship was in Plymouth or Southampton and Mum went to London for the day to try and see him. They met briefly and she decided we should make for Tring, which was Granny's old home and where they could probably find friends. It took her all night to get back to us at Shenfield. Dunkirk had fallen and all the London platforms were littered with returning troops. Mum kept herself busy lighting cigarettes for them, and talking to them. War is a great leveller.

Next day we were on the road again. It was a boiling hot summer day and we nearly expired from heat packed in, as we were. Mum tried to drive to Tring which sounds easy enough except that every signpost had been removed, as had every Church notice board or, in fact, anything which would tell an invading army where they were. People were very afraid of giving directions and many times we found ourselves chasing after policemen for help. Mum bought a compass and I sat beside her keeping it pointing north. Suddenly Granny and Mum recognised familiar landmarks and we were there. We looked in vain for some of Granny's friends. Finally we found a lady at the village of Wiggington at the top of Oddy Hill who was prepared to give us board and lodging. We had two bedrooms, and a small sitting-cum-dining room. We were adequately fed, and as Mother had little to do she got herself a job in the bank in Tring. Once again our education was entrusted to a woman from the village. It must have been difficult for her trying to educate us with Granny sitting by the fire doing the mending, and the budgie expounding his vocabulary. Thus we edgily survived through the winter of 1940/41 and the Battle of Britain was in full swing. Mum drove to the bank each day and at night parked her car on the hill, carefully removing the rotor arm. One night she saw someone flashing semaphore signals from the hill and reported it to the police. We never knew whether it was a spy. I remember little of the war at that time because my own life was seeing changes. I started to walk up the village, first to the letterbox, and then to the church. It was very Anglo Catholic for a village church and I found myself telling the vicar about my faith and my experience at the convent, and of my desire to become a convert and my fear of hurting my mother. He showed me how I could embrace the whole Catholic faith without changing my church allegiance. I seldom got to Church as it was really too far for me to go on my own, but it changed the way I thought and prayed.

From the corner of the green there was a wood that led down into Tring. A short way down there was a derelict summerhouse overlooking the road. I have told you of our fascination with the princess's house at Windsor. Here was our chance. By now we had made friends with some of the village kids who played on the hill and I could walk a bit. We now moved in, in force, "borrowing" hammer and nails and bits of wood from children's fathers who had gone to fight for king and country. For weeks we had a wonderful time until one day we found a fence built all round the place. It was to be a private retreat for Dame Peggy Ashcroft.

My mother's brother was having some marital trouble and wanted her to have his children to live with us for the time being. They came, but there was obviously no room for us at the house in Wiggington. Mum was keeping us solvent working at the bank and she had a longing that we should try and get into her old school at Berkhamsted. She soon found a large house for rent which was a short distance from the school. By now the Battle of Britain was in full swing. Unfortunately Berkhamsted could not take us as they were overfull. However, they used the school buildings only in the morning, There was another school, South Hampstead High, which, like Berkhamsted, was part of the Girls Public Day School Trust, and had the buildings in the afternoon. Most of the pupils were evacuees and lived in billets. They agreed to take me at my mother's risk, and in September 1941, at the age of fourteen, I started to experience the rough and tumble, and the discipline of full school life. We had lessons from 2 to 6 p.m. each day. The mornings were given over to games and prep which could be done in a big hall in the garden called the Steed room, for those who for any reason could not work in their billet.

At the age of fourteen I didn't take too kindly to being pushed to school each day in a wheelchair. Also, Sheila began to dislike having to push me. The problem was overcome by dint of my having made a very special and understanding friend, Ines. She was very sporty and strong, and was soon wheeling me to school each day perched on her bicycle and clutching both our school satchels and often a large amount of her sports gear. She became expert at wheeling this enormous weight up and down hill and I got very expert at balancing. I never came off. She very soon mastered my timetable as well as her own, and when the bell went between lessons would rush to take me to my next lesson, before going to hers. The staff members were understanding and never commented if she arrived late.

We became very firm friends. Often the siren would go during lessons and she would rush to escort me to the basement where the whole school would assemble until the all clear. Each day we prayed at assembly for those who had been bereaved or injured in the bombings in London, Liverpool and Coventry, and still the invasion did not come. Instead, Russia came into the war and invaded Poland. Then Japan came in on the side of Germany and Italy and was foolish enough to bomb Pearl Harbour and bring America in. Although after Dunkirk the USA had supplied us with weapons and planes, they had so far managed to remain neutral. This was no longer possible. The whole world was at war, or so it seemed.

In Berkhamsted we were probably as safe as anywhere. A German bomber came down in a field close by and the pilot was interned. We all rushed out to get sections of the parachute and Mum made us all underclothes from it. I have still got a bit of it. On another occasion the main water pipe burst. This supplied most of the houses in Berkhamsted and everyone, including the doctors, got severe dysentery. My Aunt Eileen and her young son came from another part of the country to nurse us. We had to get all drinking water from a standpipe in the town but the budgie died and the dog was ill. As soon as she could go back to work, Mum brought bottles of water back from Tring. Once again my life was threatened—but the Guinea Pig survived.

By now food was very strictly rationed. We largely lived on vegetables and Granny fed us a lot on thick soup. We bought dried egg powder in a tin for cooking as there were no eggs in town, unless one was lucky enough to know someone who kept their own chickens. The meat ration was minute and allowed about one meal a week and fish was practically non-existent except for a few freshwater fish, which were bought on the black market. I well remember our first Christmas in Berkahmsted when Dad sent us a tin of chicken from Scarpa Flow in Scotland where his boat was, and we gratefully shared it among six of us. The worst part of the rationing for me was bread rationing. It went on for years and long after the end of the war. I still think bread and buns are my favourite food, and like many people of my age, cannot bear to see even a mouthful of food wasted. One has to be really hungry for a long time to really appreciate the gift of food.

While I was still recovering from dysentery, a neighbour of my paternal grandparents, who were still in Clacton, rang to say that she had found my grandmother had died in her bed and my grandfather was very ill. Granny took the call and sent the police for my mother who went off to Clacton where she remained until after the funeral. There was an inquest and it was found that they had both been quite ill with 'flu and in the depression which often follows this illness, and with the struggle to keep them going in wartime, Grandpa's nerves had given way and he had given them both an overdose. It was only the fact that their neighbour had popped in to see how they were that Grandpa survived. He was in a mental hospital until well after the end of the war.

5
EXAMS

My father spent the early years of the war in a frigate going down the African coast on his way to Australia. He spent some time at Mombassa and at Cape Town where there is no doubt he enjoyed himself, having little knowledge of how we were suffering at home. He wrote regularly and kept a diary of his travels, which I still have. Then we were informed that he had become a 'Brass hat.' This meant he had been given a Command and was able to put the famous commanders laurel leaves round his hat and have three rings round his sleeve. We were very proud of him. It also meant he was to see a lot more of the war. His first command was to the parent ship of the destroyer fleet at Scarpa Flow. The Christmas of 1941, when we were giving thanks for our tinned chicken, he was entertaining the King on his ship.

Mother never trusted his fidelity—not without good reason—and when the following year she had to go to London on business, she bumped into him in Westminster. She said he looked guilty and barely spoke to her. She came back very upset, imagining he had been with a lady friend. It turned out he had a great deal of responsibility equipping the ships that were to transport the troops across the channel on D-day. He was terrified that if he spoke to Mother, someone would spot him and think he was giving away national secrets.

The lease ran out on our house in Berkhamsted, my uncle remarried and his children left to live with their new young stepmother. My mother left the bank and we found a house to let at Ashley Green. This house had a big garden and an orchard. We joined the Young Farmers Club and together with many young people were given day-old calves to rear. We called them Diddle and Nan after our two favourite teachers. Nan sadly died within a few days, but Diddle thrived and at six months joined the other heifers at the farm. The bullocks were slaughtered. Were we glad we had a heifer! Mother managed to get one or two hens, which we let run in the Orchard. We also got some rabbits. Make no mistake about it—we cared for them all well but lost no sleep about having them killed to supplement our diet. It seems incredible to me now, but I had no qualms at all about skinning, cooking and eating the friendly little bunnies I had been cuddling the day before. War and hunger does strange things to the best of us! We got a cockerel, hatched out chicks, grew fresh vegetables and enjoyed life in the lull between the bombing and the doodlebugs. Although we knew the enemy was as near as the Channel Islands, most of the fighting was on the Russian border. I was doing well, and, as Ines was not very happy in her billet, she came to live with us. With her help I could manage to catch the bus down to school. Finishing school at six o'clock meant travelling home in the blackout; we learnt the hymn "Lead kindly light" and kept up our spirits singing it while trundling home from the bus stop.

In November 1942 I was confirmed with the rest of my class. The church in Ashley Green was near enough for me to walk there and I joined the choir and started helping with the Sunday School. Although she was Jewish, Ines enjoyed the choir and sometimes came with me. I enjoyed the Confirmation instruction and, as I had learnt the Catholic catechism, found learning the one in the prayer book a cinch. We were told that we would probably not feel anything on the day, and not to be disappointed as it was not about feeling. We wore our school uniform and white veils and were sad that wartime precluded the white dresses. I compensated for this later by making white dresses for both my daughters for their confirmations! I think it sad that the white dresses and veils are no longer the norm. The bridal dress and the veil make the day special for most brides, and I believe it would do much to make Confirmation special for many girls if more effort were made to help them feel and look like the bride of Christ. I think there were about forty of us and we each had to answer the Bishop when our names were called.

"Margaret Anne Adams."

"I do."

It took ages and I longed for the moment when the Bishop would put his hand on my head and I would receive the Holy Spirit. I was well prepared not to feel anything but I started to shake as though I had a high fever. I returned to my seat still quaking and my teacher and friends got quite worried. I believe to this day that it was the Baptism of the Holy Spirit, although we did not hear about it then as much as now. Afterwards I compared notes with some of my friends, and many others had had the same experience to greater or lesser degree, though none of us would have dreamt of telling an adult. I made my First Communion a week later at Ashley Green.

Once again we had to move. The owner of "The Orchard" wanted to sell and various people came to look with a view to buying. We were all thrilled when the great David Niven came to view and actually kissed my calf Diddle on the end of her soft nose! Mum had had to make several journeys to Clacton to sort out my grandparents' bungalow. She was anxious not to sell while Dad was away and had decided to let. My Aunt Eileen had been working as a prep school matron in order to give her son a good education. Now that he was away at a public boarding school, she wanted to realise her life's ambition to run a nursing home and the house at Clacton would make a start until she found something larger. As we had to get out of "The Orchard" Granny decided to go and make her home with her.

The school in Hampstead was reopened and, as the threat of invasion seemed unlikely and bombing became a thing of the past, many children were returning to London. Mum decided to look for somewhere to rent near the school in South Hampstead and found a really lovely ground floor flat with a garden. We were even allowed to take the chickens, but ate the hard-worked cockerel before leaving. Before the start of term the doodlebugs started. These were unmanned aircraft known as V1s that sounded just like a plane until the engine suddenly stopped. There was seldom any air raid warning, but if one heard a plane stop, wherever one was, one dived under a hedge, into a doorway—anywhere. The fallout from these ghastly missiles was enormous and many were the cause of fires.

Sheila was re-evacuated with most of those who had returned. Once again I was a problem. No one wanted the responsibility of having me and I wanted to stay in London with my mother. However, there were very few teachers in London and, although older girls who were matriculating that year could stay at their parents' risk and go to the part of the school in Hampstead, the subjects offered were very limited. Three of my chosen subjects—Latin, Religious Education and Music—were not provided for in Hampstead, and I would have to go back to Berkhamsted to take these.

First, Sheila persuaded her hosts to take me with the six evacuees they already had. She promised faithfully she would look after and help me. It was a vile place, which smelt of stale cabbage. By now most people were livings largely on whale meat, as other meat was in extremely short supply unless you could shoot some rabbits. The song "Run, Rabbit Run" was very popular as all kinds of people tried to bag one for their supper. I wonder now, how many were injured by amateur shots and left to die agonising deaths. Anyway, we were fed very badly in this billet and it soon proved far too far from the school for me to walk or for anyone to push me on their bikes. Mum rang the couple who lived next door to us at Ashley Green and begged them to take me, as the lady was a nurse. She agreed to take me and one of my school friends until our exams. She had avoided taking evacuees because of her nursing, but was happy to have Susan and me because we were older and largely independent. From then on, it was all systems go to pass our exams. Sheila and the rest were moved from the bad digs and found better places.

It is probably worth pointing out that in those days, there were no GCSEs. We took general school certificates, which consisted of a minimum of five subjects, always including English and Maths. One had to pass in at least five subjects to obtain one's certificate. Failure meant taking the whole lot again next year. To get a Matric, you had to take a minimum of six subjects and get a credit in English, Maths, a language and two others. I sat seven, got six credits, and failed Chemistry. Several papers were done in the air raid shelter because of the rockets.

My hostess was a brilliant cook and could do really tasty things with vegetables and a few spices. Many Sunday afternoons I would wander through the woods with her, picking nettles for a salad tea. These she would mix with grated carrot, and very good they were, too. She encouraged me well and encouraged my efforts to get around and lead a normal life. I went regularly to church and taught in Sunday School and sang in the choir again. Susan, my friend who was with me, and I worked hard for our exams and were given plenty of space and opportunity to do so. Ines and I both learnt to play the piano and took our turn at playing the march which took us out of assembly back to our classes each day. As the school came from South Hampstead, about 70% of the pupils were Jewish and many had fled from Germany, the lucky ones with their parents, the rest having left their families to be massacred in Belsen or Auschwitz. Twice a week we would worship God together, using hymns and prayers, which did not mention Jesus. The rest of the week we had separate prayers and then came together for notices at the end. Senior girls were often allowed to choose the hymns and I well remember someone getting told off by a Jewish teacher for having the hymn "To mercy, pity, peace and love" at joint prayers.

"Who do you think it refers to?" the teacher asked.

"God," replied the girl.

"It refers to Jesus," said the teacher.

"It doesn't say so," said the girl. "Isn't it from one of the psalms?"—and this just goes to show everything can be what you read into it!

I was developing a rather firm but rather naive faith. I talked to God incessantly and did everything to keep Him in control of my life. For instance, if I was in doubt as to whether it was cold enough to wear a certain sweater, I would shut my eyes, pray, spin my bible around in my lap, let it open and look to see where it had opened. If in the Old Testament I had to wear the sweater; if in the New, I did not. I never doubted the results and practised it over many things. I bought a 1928 prayer book, which had every day's reading in it and I started saying that version of the divine office daily. I fasted and did everything I could to bring my troublesome body under subjection. My closest friends teased me about my boyfriend, Will Power.

One day we heard on the news that some doodlebugs had fallen on South Hampstead. We rushed to the phones. Some of the girls with parents in London were able to make contact, but some whose homes were near the school could not. We heard that the school had been only slightly damaged but, try as I might, I could not make contact with my mother. I tried to phone the local police but they were far too busy with other people trying to contact relatives. There was nothing for it but to keep trying to phone. After about four sleepless nights, during which I dreamt of never seeing Mother again, I suddenly phoned to hear her answer quite unperturbed; a doodlebug had fallen on the telegraph wires and put all of the phones out of order. We had lost our windows but Mum was all right as she had got under the billiard table when the dog warned her. As I have previously said, Bess knew the difference between the planes that were always circling overhead, looking for enemy activity and the doodlebugs. Just as many dogs will give warning of an impending thunderstorm, she was able to sense the approach of the missiles and would rush around in a frenzy until Mum picked her up and got into a safe place. Mum kept her with her day and night.

By now the fortunes of war were changing. Allied troops were recapturing France and Holland on one front, America and the third army were fighting in the dessert, and Russia was storming across eastern Germany. War seemed further and further away and that summer most of the school returned to South Hampstead. I would be able to live at home for my years in the sixth form. Some of the girls returning home had accommodation problems and a kind of evacuation in reverse took place. My Mother, having a huge flat with a high rent, gladly agreed to help out and took in five or six other girls, either those who, like Sheila, were doing their school certificate and Matric or other sixth formers. Mum looked after us extremely well. She ran a tight ship and we all worked hard as well as having a lot of fun. We were completely unknowledgable where boys were concerned; those we knew were somebody's kid brother or were in uniform and at war. Had we been a couple of years older things might have been very different as we could have gone into pubs and clubs and fraternised with the troops when on leave. For now, war and single sex schooling made that impossible. We lived out our feelings in schoolgirl crushes and very intense relationships and matured emotionally very slowly.

During the winter of 1944, we all got measles. I think some of the girls may have been temporarily housed elsewhere, as I do not remember them being around while we were ill. Sheila was very ill and delirious. There were no antibiotics in those days and all illnesses had to run their courses. Fortunately, I had it very mildly, but it was bad enough and left me with a slight deafness, which has remained with me to this day. If people drop their voices, I always miss the end of sentences and this sometimes causes them to think I have misunderstood them or am not listening. I have now learnt instinctively to sit with my good ear towards people and to guess correctly the bits I don't hear. Fortunately it has never got any worse, or I do not think it has.

I had decided to do English, Latin and Religious Knowledge for my Higher School Certificate (now known as A-levels). I think I only chose Latin because Ines was doing it and we both had a crush on the teacher. One of the Latin papers was on Roman history, which was extremely badly taught, and as a result, I ended failing Latin, which meant I never did get my Higher Schools. I did get a credit in English and a distinction in R.K. but it didn't count. I also got a special mention for coming top in the country in my choice of third paper, "The history of thought between the Old and New Testaments." I don't think many people took that paper but I had a fascination with the Apocrypha and the history of that era, and still have.

In the spring of 1945, war with Germany was fast coming to an end. On one particular day forever in the history books, we wandered round the school trying to concentrate on our studies when towards the end of the afternoon, the whole school was called to assembly. The headmistress told us that war with Germany was over. There was an outbreak of cheering and, whether from emotion, stress or relief, I do not know, but several other girls and I dropped in a dead faint and had to be carried back to our classrooms. Thank goodness it was a Friday, and there was no school the next day.

6

THE GUINEA PIG GOES TO COLLEGE

The VE celebrations went on all weekend. We went from Hampstead to the West End two nights running. Two things stand out in my mind, standing on an island in the middle of the road when Winston Churchill went past in an open carriage. He looked straight at us and gave the famous V sign. The other memory is of nearly getting pushed under a train trying to get home on the underground. Some people were pushed off the platform and sadly lost their lives having survived the war. The pressure of the crowd behind as each full train came in was enormous, and those in the front had to be held by those behind to keep them from falling. Trains ran all night, every minute or two, to get people home.

A few days after our celebrations we received news from Father. He was in the thick of the dreadful war off the coast of Japan. He seemed very depressed, as he believed war could well go on out there for many more years. It is impossible in many ways to justify Hiroshima and Nagasaki, but without the atom bomb he might well have been right. Dad, who later brought home a ship full of prisoners of war, who would not have survived many more days, let alone years, had no doubt at all about the rightness of it and I never discussed my feelings with him.

Like everyone else, I had been called up at sixteen, but like everyone else pursuing education, was excused war service. Now I was eighteen and so was called up again. Girls had a choice between each of the three women's branches of the services, or being a land girl or nursing. I said nothing about my heart trouble, not realising that everyone had a medical, and, as I did not think I could survive the land army, put down for nursing. Of course I was exempt on medical grounds and was green with envy when eighteen months later Sheila did her stint in the land army. Conscription went on for girls for quite a time and for lads for many years.

I was eighteen in the summer of 1945 and was the eldest in the Lower VIth, being about a year behind because of the amount of schooling I had missed. During the summer months the girls in the VIth form were allowed to lie on a piece of roof outside the first floor landing to study. That is, everyone except me was allowed out. It was only about four feet from the ground and not dangerous for girls of their age, but was presumed dangerous for me. For a time a friend would stay in with me, as it seemed to them unfair I should get left out. One day no one wanted to stay in, so they contrived to get me through the window and sit all round me so that I would not get spotted, nor could I possibly slip off even if I turned giddy. On about the third such adventure we were found out, the others were told off and I was sent to the head. My punishment was to be told that I could not be a prefect in the Upper VIth. There were seven of us in the Upper VIth the following year, the head girl, vice head, four prefects and me—and all because I went on that damned roof! The injustice of it still stays with me and quite spoilt my last year at school. I have thought since that this was God's way of giving me a lesson in humility, a virtue I sadly lacked.

As I have said, many of my friends had escaped from Europe and from Hitler's ethnic cleansing before the war and were hoping to be reunited with relatives. Instead, we would go to the pictures and see the horrible sights of the opening up of the death camps. Or we would go to the Home Office and try to find out whether people's parents had survived. I do not remember hearing of one person who had survived, although I know some did. The girls varied in how they handled their loss. Some wanted to be naturalised British and lose their European identity, although most were very proud of their Jewish ancestry. Of course, a number did marry Englishmen. Others joined the Zionist movement and went to Israel. Our head girl was one of these. Others emigrated to the States or Canada. Ines' father was a famous music conductor and had somehow managed to escape internment, and her mother was a dentist. Soon after the war they got itchy feet and went to see what life was like in Canada. The next year Ines and her grandmother went out to join them.

It was some months after VJ day that Dad was due to come home. I do not know all the facts but Mum had opened some letters from various girl friends and was convinced he was not hurrying home. As these ladies were ones he had met in the early part of the war in South Africa and he had for the last three years been at Scarpa or in the Far East, it did not seem likely to me. His excuse when he wrote was that as he was on the parent ship of the destroyer fleet and could not leave until all the other ships were safely back—which seemed reasonable enough. I do not know what they had said to one another in their letters, but Dad started writing to me rather than Mum and on the day his train was due in at Euston, Sheila and I went to meet him after asking Ines to keep an eye on Mum. When we arrived home Mother was locked in her bedroom and it was some weeks before they would speak or even be in the same room together. It was a horrible ending to the war. It seemed that when most people were celebrating the return of their menfolk, we had all this misery and tension. I found out later that this kind of thing went on in many families, and everyone was suffering from post war blues. After five years people change so much.

I think one of the things which helped Mum and Dad come together again, was that my health was once more deteriorating quite quickly. For some winters I had had very bad colds and tonsillitis, which was not helping my breathing. Our doctor suggested I have my tonsils out at a small private hospital. Strangely enough, Roman Catholic nuns ran this. The RCs always seemed to be there at the right moment for me. It was the first time I had had an anaesthetic and it was not without considerable danger. As I was wheeled along the corridor from my room to the theatre, nuns lined the corridor and offered prayers in Latin and English. It was very comforting. Anaesthetics then were not what they are today and involved having a mask put over one's face while still conscious. I dreamt that I was being chased and was trying to run away and my heart was pounding so much that it finally burst and I woke up. The operation was a success. A few hours later I haemorrhaged and had to go back to theatre. I begged the doctor to let me die rather than put me through that chase again. He ignored my pleas, stitched my tonsils, and I lived. I only once experienced that chase again and that was when I had to have a tooth out. Thank God for the injection in the back of the hand—it is so much less traumatic.

As soon as I had recovered from my tonsillectomy I was raring to go to college. It was extremely difficult to get into any college that year as so many people whose education had been disrupted by war service had first claim. As I have said, I failed my Higher School Certificate but did get very good marks for R.I. There was just a chance I might be accepted to read theology. Doctors were now talking in terms of another three or four years. Theology seemed a very good preparation for life or death. I was accepted and started that October. My darling father spent his war gratuity on my tonsillectomy and my college fees to the theological department of Kings College, London. I was very blessed.

I enjoyed every minute of my life at Kings. The theological department is on the 3rd floor and I was given keys to the service lift so that I was free to go up and down as I wished. Sometimes Dad took me to college by car, but mostly I went on the number 13 bus, which ran from the end of our road to just outside college. I suffered a lot of chest pain, which also made my arms, and legs have pins and needles or go quite numb. This could be quite frightening at times, but I found it could be relieved if someone massaged my wrists, and I would often sit in lectures with a friend each side trying to rub my wrists in between taking notes. I copied their notes later. Determined not to miss one moment of my life, I joined the college choir, the local church youth club, the Church choir and went with Dad to a London Choral Society. I have never been able to understand it, but I had more control over my breathing when singing than at any other time. I am sure it helped me a lot.

Most of the men in the department were training to be ordinands, and those not doing degrees were doing the General Ordination exam, as well as becoming associates of the college (A.K.C.). There were over 200 of them and some of them had just returned from the war. A few were in quite a bad way. I well remember one chap who kept bottles of milk in his locker and had to have a few ounces of milk every hour. He had been a prisoner of war of the Japanese, and his stomach had become so shrunken from starvation that he could not tolerate ordinary food, and had to have regular milk feeds day and night like a baby. He did improve but it was a long, slow process.

There were only about twenty of us girls in the faculty. Some wanted to teach and the rest of us wanted to be Parish Workers or Moral Welfare Workers. Our exam was called the Inter Diocesan Certificate and had to be taken in Theology and at least one other part—either Youth work, Moral Welfare, Education, or Pastoralia. As these latter four demanded some practical work, it seemed doubtful whether I would ever get the needed qualifications. I battled on with the theology part and attended the A.K.C. lectures.

Social life at college was good. I joined the Student Christian Movement and went to some of their conferences, including one at Swanwick shortly after the war, which I well remember. Some very young prisoners, members of Hitler's Youth, and probably only about 16 or 17, had not been repatriated yet, and were still held in prefabricated buildings in the grounds. We went down after supper one night to have a singsong with them. We ended by singing Silent Night, we in English, they in German. I do not think there was a dry eye to be found. We wanted to hug them but were not allowed to touch them.

Rationing was still going on and I was often hungry. Our bread coupons were called BUs and had to be given up for any bread, cakes or buns. One day I was so hungry I spent my whole week's supply of BUs on a bag of buns and sat on the Number 13 bus going home and ate the lot. The college refectory where we had our lunch every day reeked of fish as we were offered whale meat stew, whale meat sausages, whale meat cutlets, whale meat mince or cheese salad. Despite the fact that you needed binoculars to see the cheese I usually had cheese salad (with extra potato which was not rationed). About this time Joe Lyons was introducing "The Salad Bowl" into his famous Corner House. Here you paid a flat charge and could then eat as much salad as you wanted. There was one such establishment in the Strand and we would go there with friends in the evening before going home and stuffing ourselves, going back for refills again and again. The salads were wonderful and varied and often there were eggs as well!

I made many friends at college and was treated as one of the gang as far as possible. It has been good to follow the fortunes of a number of friends who have done well for themselves and become famous as Bishops or Deans. There were three of us women who knocked about together; one became a teacher, and the other, like me, a priest. While at college I encountered politics for the first time, starting in the Young Conservatives, as they had a very good social life and the best dances. My mother was as blue as they come and my father, after a brief flirtation with Oswald Mosley before the war, believed, after the war, that Winston Churchill was second only to God. His disgust when the country threw Churchill out was unspeakable. It never at first occurred to me to be anything other than Tory. That was before I joined the Student Christian Movement and was dyed bright red. I longed to haul down the class structures and rebuild a very different Britain. I was very interested in many of the new ideas. The PAYE tax reform, the plans for a free health service, nationalisation of the roads and railways and the essential services all seemed wonderful and plain common sense to me. I sang the Red Flag for quite a few years.

During our time in the VIth form, and after, when she was studying classics at Bedford College and I was at Kings, Ines and I remained firm friends. We had lots of discussion about our different beliefs. I found that she and her family seemed to know little about their religion although they had suffered so much in Germany from being Jewish. This worried me and I wanted Ines to know God, whether the God of Abraham or Jesus did not at first matter. I just wanted her to know God so that she could share more of the things which were special to me. I was curious to know more about her beliefs and we started going together to the Liberal Synagogue in St. John's Wood on Saturdays and to Holy Trinity Finchley Road, where we were in the youth club, on Sundays. This went on for quite a while. I found the Synagogue fascinating and learnt the Shema and some of the Jewish prayers by heart. Ines, however, seemed much more drawn to the Church and questioned me endlessly. One day she asked me what one had to do to become a Christian and whether it was possible for a Jewess to do so. There was a sister organisation to the C.M.S. called the C.M.J. or Christian Mission to Jews and which worked among Hebrew Christians in all parts of the world. I talked to them and one day suggested to Ines that all she had to do was to ask Jesus into her life and this would not in any way affect her Jewish nationalism of which she was then very proud. One morning just before we left school she came to me and said she had given herself to Jesus in the bath. We have laughed over this many times since. The next step was to tell Ines' parents. They were understanding, blamed themselves for not attending to their daughter's spiritual needs (the fault of many parents, I feel), and said they would not stand in her way as long as she had a course of instruction from a rabbi before being baptised. To Ines' great credit she went faithfully to her instruction for many months without appearing to once waver in her Christian commitment. She then had to start on her preparation for baptism and confirmation. Sadly, I was to be in hospital for both these events.

At the start of my second year at Kings, I began to worry about what was going to happen to me next. I was in my twenty-first year and wanted to take hold of my life and have some direction. Various ideas were put forward by my parents, tutors and friends, one of which was that I should work in a Christian bookshop where my theological knowledge might be put to good use; another was that I should help in some way with the training of Sunday School teachers. However, my health was very unreliable. Some days I could cope with quite a tough schedule, while on others I was in pain and could barely stand. God was preparing his Guinea Pig.

Dad, now back at work at the Bank, came home one day and pointed out an article in his paper which said that a certain Dr. Blalock who had been operating in America on the arteries and veins leading to the heart, was coming to England at the end of the year and was to show his technique to the heart consultant Russell Brock at Guys Hospital. These operations were very expensive and, of course, this was before the days of a National Health Service. Mother and dad counted their pennies but refused to raise any hope in me. However, the Bank of England were contributors to the work of Guys Hospital and all their employees paid into an insurance scheme with the hospital. All my medical expenses could be met, as it turned out, and in January I went in to see if I was a suitable candidate for a Blalock operation. I was considered unsuitable for reasons I will attempt to explain, but at the end of a week Mr. Brock, as he was then (later he was knighted and then given a peerage for his heart surgery), came and said, "Don't be upset, old thing. I am hoping to start operating on the open heart before the end of the year and you will be one of my first patients."

I was born with what is known in medical circles as a Fallot's Tetralogy. There are two causes for babies being born as what is normally called 'blue babies.' Before birth the baby's blood passes down the placenta to the mother to be oxygenated. At the moment of birth, when the baby breathes, the blood flows through the pulmonary artery from the baby's heart to the lungs where it gets re-oxygenated. Then it passes through the pulmonary vein back to the heart for re-circulating around the body. In some patients the pulmonary artery doesn't open or only half opens. Also, before birth, the little ductus arteriosus or small vein which bypasses the baby's lungs before birth should shrivel up and fibrose. In other patients, the pulmonary artery does not open at all and the ductus can remain operational, which is what had happened to me. In both cases there were other problems arising from the condition. The heart becomes enlarged and changes position in the body and a hole is forced, allowing bad blood to leak through to the good and causing the blue colour. (All babies are blue at birth and usually turn pink when they start to live on their own heart and lungs). The Blalock operation was considered suitable for some as this operation did not involve cutting into the wall of the heart at all. But no operation could be performed on me unless my heart was cut into.

I was grateful to have it all explained to me by Lord Brock and as some of the operations done by Dr. Blalock did not seem too successful and children had died, I was quite happy to wait. I returned to college, passed the theology part of my I.D.C. and got my A.K.C. Then followed one of the most wonderful and yet most devastating weekends of my life. Wonderful, because it was my twenty-first birthday; devastating, because I was leaving Kings. A committee drawn from each of the six faculties in turn ran the whole college. This year it was the turn of the 'Theologs.' One of our activities was to organise the end of year dance, which was to take place on the Friday before the end of term (which also happened to be the eve of my twenty first). I, of course, went quite prepared to spend the evening watching the dancing. The custom was for the head of the Students' Union, this year, of course a theologian, to start the dancing, and I could hardly believe it when he came to me, helped me to my feet and started to lead me round the floor. I was very giddy and fell over his feet, but neither he or I seemed to care. He continued to be very attentive to me and later told the whole college that it was my birthday, how my life hung in the balance and how I needed everyone to pray for me.

The next day was my birthday and we all went out for a family meal and a West End film. On Sunday the celebrations continued at church and on the Monday my parents gave me the most fabulous birthday party. Mum fixed up suitable lighting in the wide hall of our spacious flat and somehow came by loads of great 40's music, rock and roll and lovely Bing Crosby and Frank Sinatra smoochy numbers. All my college friends came and the college chaplain, the great Sid Evans (who later became College Dean and then Dean of Salisbury) organised games and competitions. I had so many presents it was completely overwhelming. I feel that I never showed enough gratitude to anyone, especially to my parents. It is one of those things I have been kicking myself about since their death.

Two days later I left Kings. The memories were wonderful. The future was very bleak.

7

DEATH AND RESURRECTION

During the summer holidays I had time to think and to panic. There was no doubt that my condition was deteriorating and all my hopes were pinned on getting that vital call to Guy's Hospital to see if anything could be done to save me. Sheila had gone to University Hospital in London to train to be a nurse. Nursing or veterinary nursing had always been among my dreams. Ines was going back to college where she was studying classics. Had she not been at college she would have already gone to Canada with her parents, but was now living with her grandmother while she got her classics degree. She was now well established in her local church at St. John's Wood and was being prepared for Baptism and Confirmation. However, I knew that it was only a matter of time before our lives would go their separate ways. I had depended on her so much to keep me thinking positively. It seemed that when I was with her I could go up to London, go to her father's concerts with her, have fun and do all the things that people of my age wanted to do. She had even taken me to sleep on the roadside outside the Whitehall theatre to watch the procession and join in the relayed service when Princess Elizabeth married the dashing Philip Mountbatten. We also now shared our Christian faith, which was very important to us both. She and her family always made me feel normal, while at the same time looking after me. I already missed her parents and was soon to miss her. I had to do something or I would have gone mad.

One day Ines and I went into the S.P.C.K. bookshop in Northumberland Avenue and I asked if they would give me a job. They had no vacancies in their shop but could offer me a job in their accountancy department. This involved opening the mail, collecting and entering the cheques and money orders and filling in and posting the official receipts. It meant typing, but only using capital letters. As my typing was a two-finger effort, I was very slow and often stayed on to do overtime at my own expense, as I was so grateful to be given a job. Some mornings I was so unwell after the bus ride in, that I had to lie down for an hour before starting work, and the whole department was delayed waiting for the post. They were so patient with me.

While working overtime one evening the phone rang rather persistently and, after some hesitation, I answered it. It was my father to say he had just got home from work to find a letter asking whether I could go into Guys immediately. It was already about 7.00pm so, if I was to go in that day, there was no time for me to go home. My mother and Sheila were both away, so I agreed with Dad that he would ring the hospital to say I was on my way. I asked him to pack up my night things and a few bits and pieces, collect me from work and take me in. I then bustled round to leave everything in the office as organised as possible, and left a letter to my boss on my desk saying "Goodbye". Then began five weeks of tests. I had catheters pushed up the veins of my arms and legs into and through my heart. I also had dye injected through my body under X-ray. At one time my arms had been so cut about that they both had to be splinted, and I had to sit by a bedridden patient for her to feed me my dinner. There were two younger girls on the ward having similar tests. It was 1948, the year of the great polio outbreak, and there were two "iron lungs" on the ward which rumbled day and night, and in a kind of conservatory built on the side of the ward were three TB patients. In a bed at the end of the ward was Pat, the hospital almoner, who herself had caught Polio. She'd been for a few days in a "lung", but had recovered apart from her legs. In a vain hope to get these working again they needed to be put in a swing over her bed every few hours and swung. I tried to help her and the busy nurses by swinging her legs. It was a hopeless task and she got very depressed. Trying to keep her going stopped me worrying about myself.

One morning we were being woken on the ward with a cup of tea when Pat called across the ward, "It's a boy!" She had her earphones on to listen to the 6.00am news. Princess Elizabeth had had a son, and we all drank the health of the new prince in rather tepid hospital tea.

At the end of the five weeks the physician, under whose care I was put while having the tests in this medical ward, came in, pulled the curtains round the bed, and sat down. This was it! Very gently and kindly he told me that my heart was far too damaged to survive such an untried operation and I could go home the next day. I was completely devastated. For a few moments my faith was gone, and thoughts of jumping out of the bathroom window raced through my brain. As I rushed past Pat's bed in the direction of the bathroom she called me back and asked me what Dr. Baker had said. Talking to her helped me to see things in perspective. I was ready to live for as long as God willed it and to die when he decided it was time. Also, my friend Will Power returned. Pat was also feeling depressed about her future and we cried together, but I went to bed quite calm and looking forward to going home next day.

Early next morning Sir Russell Brock came to see me. "Well, old thing," he said, "I've decided you would be a very good candidate for my new operation. You have, I think, about 75% chance of surviving the operation and about 50% of being better. Do you want to take the chance?" One thing about Sir Russell, he never beat about the bush! My first thought was of about the other 25% if there was no improvement and I was still alive. This was worrying. I asked him what could happen then. It seems I could be not very different or I could have brain damage or be paralysed. I had no doubt that I wanted the operation, and the rest was up to God. He then said that as I was going down so quickly the sooner the better and he would operate in ten days. Did I want to stay in hospital or go home for a week? As my parents were coming to get me that day in any case, I decided to go home. I have wondered many times why the two doctors did not get their act together before talking to me. The extremes of emotions I suffered in those two days were quite unnecessary, but I suppose it would have been worse if my hopes had been first raised and then dashed. I think there was a feeling among the doctors that some of the heart surgeons were looking for human guinea pigs, which in a sense they were, but in most of our cases our lives were over anyway. As far as I was concerned, I believed that God was telling me to trust him and not to put so much faith in my Will Power. He was making me submissive and humble.

It was quite a week. First I got a sniffle and my good intentions of doing my Christmas shopping had to be aborted while I stayed in and nursed my cold. I wrote my cards, putting in a covering note to say goodbye to my friends in case I didn't survive. Quite a few visitors came to see me and I realised I was going to be in hospital for Ines' Baptism and Confirmation. Sod's law!!

The following Monday I returned, this time to the surgical ward, for the operation on Thursday. There were two ops a week, one on a Monday and one on a Thursday. Each one would take about nine hours. As I was being admitted, the Monday patient returned from the theatre and was put in the plastic tent. She was alive, at least. Doris and I later became great friends. She had a Blalock operation and later was to become the first person to have a baby after heart surgery. Although still in the tent, Doris was so much better the next day that it gave me real hope. I learned that the other patients in the ward all got very anxious every time a heart patient went to theatre. As the nine hours went by, the ward would become very quiet. If the patient was not going to come back, sister would announce it to the ward at suppertime and the quiet would remain all evening. One evening sister brought me a letter from Pat, still in the medical ward, wishing me well.

On Tuesday the chaplain came to see me. Special prayers were being said for me in Southwark Cathedral and in the hospital chapel. He said he would come back that evening after the ward was quiet to hear my Confession and would bring me Communion early on Wednesday morning. Then on Wednesday evening after the nurses had got me all ready for the op., which was to start at 6.00am on Thursday, he would come and anoint me and give me last rites in case I did not come back. He was quite wonderful and popped in several times a day, sometimes just to see my visitors or to encourage the nurses, and I realise now what a difficult job he had, and how well he did it.

My parents never wavered in their support for me, but I think they may have talked over their fears with our family doctor who had become quite a friend.

All I know is that on the Wednesday evening, when I had said goodbye to my parents and had been bathed and dressed in a sterile gown and prepared for the operation, and was quietly waiting for the last visit from the Chaplain, my GP arrived, sat on my bed and begged me not to go through with it as I was being very unfair to my parents. They would have to look after me if I became paralysed or was brain damaged. They had lost their son and wanted to keep me as long as possible. I was devastated, and said I would talk to the chaplain, who then arrived. We talked and prayed and again he was quite wonderful. He promised he would support my parents, reassured me, and then gave me God's healing. By the time the nurse arrived to give me a sleeping tablet I was asleep. She still woke me and insisted on me having it! At 5.30 I was given a pre-med and a tablet to dry my mouth. This gave me some idea of what it must be like to die of thirst; my whole mouth swelled and my tongue seemed glued to the top of my mouth. The porters came and I was carted off to the mask and that fearful chase, only this time my heart did not pound. Instead, I went down a long corridor further and further, where it got brighter and brighter and I saw Colin. He was not a ten-week old baby but, somehow, I never expected he would be. I knew it was Colin because he looked just like the photos I had of Dad as a youth, and he spoke to me. He told me that I could not come any further and I had got to go back up the tunnel and it would all be all right. He told me God had a lot of work for me to do for him and that I was going to live for a very long time. Then I started to be sucked back up the tunnel and everything went black. When I opened my eyes all I could see was a square of ceiling and a square to the side through which faces peered. I saw my mother's face and then a nurse's. There was a terrifying rumbling noise going on all the time and every now and then an avalanche. I was in a completely opaque tent, the ward having run out of transparent ones, and the noise was the oxygen cylinder, and the avalanche was the ice moving about. Beside every tent was a tank of ice designed to keep the tents cool. These had to be topped up with fresh ice two or three times every day. It was always dreadfully hot in the tent and I was often terrified the ice had given out and they had forgotten to fill it up. I could not move my legs and one was in a splint attached to a drip giving me blood. Also, my left arm was paralysed and all I could move was my thumb and first finger. People came and did various things to me and from their conversations I gradually gathered that I had "died" on the table, been hastily returned to the ward before the operation had been finished to Sir Russell's satisfaction, and had been unconscious for over thirteen hours. Everyone seemed mightily relieved that I did not appear brain damaged. Only time would tell about everything else. My poor parents had been taken to the chapel and been told I was unlikely to make it and, as I would undoubtedly be a vegetable, to pray I died quickly. They had got to the underground when Mum remembered she had left her pools coupon on my locker so they came back. It was when Mum took a last look at me that I opened my eyes and recognised her and she called the nurse. It was some time after that before they left, and then they went to the phone box to ring all the family with the good news.

The next day I had excruciating pain in my back, which was to go on for days. They gave me Codeine, which was useless, and I suffered day and night and could think of little else. In those days they did not put in drains and it was the fluid building up from the operation. On the third day they drew the fluid off, through my back, a very painful procedure which I had to endure several times.

It was over and I was alive and each day was going to become better, but I knew that I could never go through it again. After a week I was taken out of the tent and sat out of bed in a chair. I promptly passed out and was put back to bed for another week, but not back in the tent. The feeling had come back in my legs and my left arm was starting to tingle and I could use my fingers. I had daily physiotherapy and on Christmas Day I walked for the first time, from my bed to the lunch table!

On the Monday after my operation the youngest of the children who had been in the medical ward with me, a little girl of six, went down for a Blalock op., and in the evening sister put her head into my tent and told me she was not coming back. There was no op on the Thursday but the following Monday the other girl, aged thirteen, went for a similar operation to me and did extremely well, getting over it remarkably quickly. I think they were waiting to see how I did before embarking on that op. again. She, Doris and I, all enjoyed our hospital Christmas together. Heart surgery was going forward in leaps and bounds, but it still seemed a complete lottery.

Two days before my operation a married woman had been admitted to the ward. She was to have had an operation, so far untried. She was not a blue baby but had a Mitral Stenosis, which had made her very handicapped. Her only hope for a normal life was to have heart surgery. She knew the operation carried great risks and was curious about the entire ministry I was having from the chaplain. She had also witnessed my miraculous recovery. She went home for Christmas and then came back to be another guinea pig. We talked a lot and the chaplain gave both her and her husband some instruction and then admitted them to Communion, and we all received the Sacrament together. She was also anointed the night before her operation. She never came back but I believe their newfound faith was a great consolation to her husband.

Two weeks after Christmas I went home prepared to live a normal life. The weakness in my left arm remained for some time but I was a lot better. My mother could not get over the fact that I was pink and I spent a lot of time lying flat on my back, which I could now do quite comfortably, to try and straighten my round shoulders. I had three desires, to smoke a cigarette, to ride a bike, and to swim. The first was easy to achieve and as I was still feeling the stress of such massive surgery, I started smoking quite heavily. The bike riding would come later. After about six weeks at home I was vacuuming the sitting room when I felt a terrible pain. I was rushed to the doctor and from him to hospital with pleurisy. Once again I had to be aspirated and was in hospital for another fortnight.

When I was better I wanted to start earning again. I could not go back to S.P.C.K. and Gilmore House Deaconess training college had agreed to take me to finish my I.D.C. but I would have to be there for two years as one could not start any work in the Church until one was twenty-four years old. Term did not start until October. This left the whole summer to fill.

Vida, my aunt, was very poorly. She had recently had a very painful operation, and had to spend quite a lot of time resting. She had two small children and my poor mother had been trying to help with them as well as me. It was suggested that I go and spend the summer with them in Leatherhead, to help out and look after the children. This worked extremely well and I was able to find gradually what I could do. I could take the children out and could push a pushchair. I could lift saucepans and cook dinners. I could stand on steps to clean windows. All this was quite a new world to me and I pushed myself hard, glorying in each new achievement. Vida slowly improved and we all had a wonderful summer together.

I returned to London in time to get ready to go to Gilmore House. I entered there and embarked on my new healthy life in the same month that Ines started her new life in Canada.

8

THE GUINEA PIG LIVES AGAIN

I entered Gilmore House full of hope and ambition, only to find I just had not learned to cope with real life. All my life I had been protected and had never experienced the ups and downs, and the cut and thrust of life. Once again I was in a completely women's world which, after life at Kings, I detested. It was like being back at school and there was very little privacy as we spent all our time in our rooms or in the library studying. The only highlight was when we went out visiting or to help with clubs, but this was only once or twice a week. Most of the women were considerably older than I and seemed to have had their fling and settled into a world of 'spinsterism' (celibates for Gods sake, no doubt). There also seemed to be a kind of Lesbian undercurrent, which I found both exciting and threatening. I was very immature because of my protected existence and was also getting delayed reaction from my operation. It often seemed that I was living in a hothouse of holiness from which I rebelled but could not get away from. I also felt my simple faith was being picked over and exposed in a way I just had not known at Kings. It was like being under an X-ray with all one's protective flesh removed and just the bones showing. There was just nowhere to hide. The discipline was strong, and we lived against a background of almost monastic rigidity with Morning Prayer, Communion, Evensong and Compline daily. We were never allowed in the chapel without putting on little veils, even wearing them to clean the chapel on Friday afternoons. I tried to be holy, and in time grew to like the security of the discipline but at first found it very hard. I loved God with all my heart but wanted to get there for myself and not because I was told to. Any discipline I had practised in the past had been self-imposed and this was not. Other people were imposing it on me. I read endless holy books, found myself a good spiritual director and tried to live up to what was expected of me.

Fortunately there was one other student, already in her second year, with whom I was able to pal up. She seemed much saner than the rest, largely, I think, because she was secretly in love with one of the curates at the parish church in Clapham. We used to walk along the common to the 8.00am service, on as many Sundays as we could, hoping that Robert would be the Celebrant. We confided a lot in one another and are still friends.

Despite this, we were in different years and doing different theological courses and I got more and more depressed. The doctor said it was delayed reaction to the shock of my operation and, after I had tried to overdose one night, I was probably lucky I was not kicked out in that first term. By Christmas I was so poorly my mother was sent for. When she arrived with Sheila, who happened to be home, I sobbed that I wanted to go back into hospital. I spent Christmas in Guys for a second year running. The other students were all very kind and kept me going with letters and gifts, and after a short course of tranquillisers I returned to Gilmore with renewed will and threw myself into my work. Because of my behaviour I was made to move out of the house into one of the overflow houses across the road where I was with two women in their 40's. At this time I also discovered the calming effect of cigarettes, which in those days were considered the panacea for all ills. The first person to offer me a cigarette was a doctor when I went to him for help with my depression. So I sat in my room drinking coffee and smoking my way through my studies.

Because I was still only twenty-two when I went to Gilmore, and I could not be licensed as a Parish Worker until I was twenty-four, I decided to stay for two years and do a Cambridge Certificate which would qualify me for teaching should I want to at a later stage. I also did my I.D.C. in Moral Welfare and Pastoralia.

I enjoyed the Moral Welfare enormously. In those days there was very little support for pregnant girls. Most went into a Mother and Baby home as soon as their pregnancy became obvious. After the baby was born the girl returned to the home and had to look after it for six weeks while she was counselled and made up her mind whether she wished to give the babe up for adoption. Most girls did. There was little support for single mothers either from the state or from their own parents. Those who could afford to help their daughters were ashamed to do so, and the rest could not afford to feed two more mouths. At six weeks the infants were offered to childless parents from the same social background and with similar characteristics. They would be fostered by the prospective parents for a further six to eight weeks, during which time the natural mother could change her mind, and if she did not, then the matter went to court and the baby was officially adopted. Although it would probably seem today a cold and heartless way of going about things, I have watched the changes over the last fifty years and still believe it was kinder to the mother and the baby than the present system of abortion, or of young girls who do not want abortion spending endless time with their children going in and out of care, as they strive to be mums before they are ready. In those days the girls were helped and befriended by the Church for a long time while they got their lives sorted out, and many of them went on to make happy and successful marriages and have more children. The children knew only one set of parents while they were young and were loved and wanted, and the decision of whether to try and find their natural parents was their own. I have seen such insecure children going back and forth from mum to foster mum for years and I cannot believe this is good. However, I'm sure there are many reading this who will violently disagree, and will point to adoptions that have broken down. All I can say is that in those days, because there were so many babies for adoption, it was far easier to match the right child to the right adopting parents, and all adopting parents had their child as a tiny baby and not, as so often happens today, as a thoroughly unsettled and disturbed toddler or school child. I also believe that when Social Services took over the welfare of mothers and babies, and the Church was no longer involved, a great deal of love and understanding was lost. I loved counselling the mums and visiting the excited childless couples to tell them we had a baby for them. There was a lot of pain but also a lot of joy. Everyone wanted the best for the new gift we had been given, the baby. I was very sad when my days with Moral Welfare ended.

For Pastoralia we were attached to a parish team and learnt visiting skills, superintending Sunday schools, sacristy work, running youth clubs, running Bible studies and confirmation classes, etc. We were sent out to a variety of parishes. I remember going one Mothering Sunday afternoon to an infant class armed with pictures of mothers doing a variety of jobs such as cooking the dinner, feeding the baby, cleaning the house, etc. For all these activities of mum we were meant to give thanks to her and to God. The class was at a church in Sloane Square. When I arrived I realised that every child had his or her "Nanny" with them and they probably only saw their mums for a few hours a day, and certainly not cooking the dinner or bathing the baby! I had to hide my pictures and improvise, but it was good training.

For my second year, because I had spent so much of my first year living out, I came back into the house again. I passed my exams and was now ready to look for my first parish.

In the summer of 1950 and halfway through my time at Gilmore, I went to work for a French dressmaker and learnt quite a bit. Clothes rationing had ended and the "New Look" was all the rage. Dresses and coats were calf length and very full. For so many years all clothes had been short and skimpy to save material, or people had been in uniform, and now everyone went mad using masses of material in long full skirts and big sleeves. It's amusing to see the fashions now in old fifties films. Food also was gradually coming off ration and most things were now back in the shops; however, we carried ration books for about five years after the war. The dressmaker taught me to make button holes on the machine, how to neaten seams, put in zips and all kinds of useful finishings which helped me later to make my own clothes and save money.

In the summer of 1951, in between going to various parishes for interviews, I decided to do a Red Cross Nursing and First Aid course. I knew I wanted to work in the East End of London and thought skills in this department might be very useful.

For some time now my parents had felt they ought to have Grandpa to live with us. Dad was very keen, and as an only child felt his responsibilities. He was trying hard to make up to Mum for his infidelities and they agreed to give it a go. I also believe that Grandpa's money was running out and it would be better all round to have him living with us. They were also anxious to buy their own house again. They had a house in Clapham, which was let at a good rent, and this would help with the mortgage. After some searching they bought a large house in Surrey. The week before we moved from Hampstead, Dad found someone else was after it, so sold it on at a much higher price, and then found a house in Springfield Road in Wallington. My parents were nothing if not good business people! How often I have wished I had inherited their business acumen. It was a big house with about six bedrooms and an enormous garden. As the plot was on a corner Dad sold the corner piece of ground with permission to build a bungalow to his specifications. Thus he paid for his big house. It gave both Sheila and me a place to call home and my maternal grandmother stayed with us for quite long periods from time to time, when she felt the need to get away from Clacton and the old people's home she helped my aunt with. My parents had an extra bathroom put in and an upstairs kitchen made and this provided me with a home when out of the parish. It was also used as a starter home by one of my cousins at one point. Mum loved the garden and made it a picture one as well as still keeping chickens. She was extremely good with my grandfather. He had always been such a creature of routine and still needed a structured life. He spent his days in the dining room reading and doing the *Telegraph* crossword. He always finished it but sometimes it took all day. Mum always saw to it that his meals were on the dot and he seemed happy enough, although he got very anxious if he ever heard them having words.

Dear little Bess was getting very old. She was dearly loved but we had had her because I was in a wheelchair. Mum felt very much that she would like to see if she could have more luck with another cocker spaniel. Bess died on September 4th 1952, and when Mum heard that a litter of spaniels belonging to a friend of a friend had been born on that day she took it for a lucky omen. Six weeks later I went home for my day off to find her cuddling a beautiful golden cocker spaniel puppy. A few weeks later I rescued a tortoise-shell kitten and the two were to be inseparable for the next 16 years. They died within a week of each other.

I finished my Red Cross lectures and then spent two weeks doing practical in a small cottage hospital in the East End. I worked on the male medical ward where most of the men were TB patients or diabetics. As the junior I spent a large part of my time testing urine or emptying and cleaning sputum mugs and urinals. Some of the men were very old but one or two were young and had been to war where they had caught TB. They were in for a long time and were determined to make the best of it. They loved to tease the nurses, and would play practical jokes on us but it was all good fun. Most of the nurses were Irish and we all lived in the nurses' home together. Considering that I was an outsider, they were very friendly and we used to go together to the RC church next to the hospital. As I had to work two Sundays I could not get to Communion. So when one of the other girls went to Confession one Saturday night, I went with her and presented myself in the confessional where I asked the priest if he would give me Communion next morning if I made my confession. As I feared he would, he flatly refused and I felt very hurt and rejected.

One afternoon I went to look at the parish of St Peter, De Beauvoir Town, not far from the hospital where I had been nursing. It was between the Kingsland Road, which ran from Islington to Dalston, and the Essex Road. All the roads led off a small London square and the church and vicarage took up one side of the square. The vicar was in his first incumbency, having been senior curate at the famous All Saints, Poplar. The parish was dead but could only go up which it seemed certain to do in this man's capable hands. He seemed keen for me to go and was interviewing soon with a view to having a deacon as well as me. He wanted us all to live in the vicarage with him, his wife, three children (then) and his aunt. It seemed a good and exciting place to start my ministry. I told him of my medical history but he was only concerned that I did the work and I agreed to start that autumn.

9
PARISH LIFE

Life at St. Peter's was a real challenge but no one could have asked for a better training. I was made sacristan and we had a daily celebration of Communion. This meant I had to be in church an hour before the service whatever time it was (on Friday we had Dockers' Mass at 5.45am!) to open up the church and put everything ready. Some days this meant chucking out drunks who had crept into the church and not been seen when the curate or I had locked up the night before. Once or twice I found one who had broken into the canteen in the crypt and then got drunk on Communion wine! However, they were harmless and always left when I said we were going to have a service. I do not ever remember having to call in the police, and mostly they just wanted somewhere to sleep.

After Mass the staff would spend an hour in private prayer and meditation and then the curate would ring the Angelus and we would say Morning Prayer. In the early days we could afford to have the heating on only on Sundays and as there were still windows missing from war damage it was bitterly cold and we prayed in scarf, gloves and a host of woollies. Then we all had a good breakfast in the Vicarage before starting work. Lunch was at 1.00pm sharp, and you were not supposed to be late without good reason. After lunch we had to rest in our rooms until 2.30. My instinct was to try and help with the washing up but there was "Auntie" and a single mother who lodged there and whose job it was to help, so I did what was expected of me. We then visited or had afternoon meetings until 5.30 when we said the Evening Office and then went to supper.

Most evenings I had clubs of one sort or another or went visiting and we all had to report to the kitchen at 10.00pm for a night drink and a sandwich. On Fridays we had staff prayers and Benediction from 10 to 11pm and did not get our night drink until after that, which made Fridays a very long day. By Saturday evening I was so tired that instead of visiting I used to come in and lie on my bed and listen to Saturday night theatre on the radio or fall asleep, after being very careful to set my alarm for just before 10 o'clock so that I did not get found out.

A lot of Saturdays I spent cleaning up the church for weddings and clearing up after as well as seeing all was ready for Sunday. One of my jobs was to see that the choirboys and servers' robes were kept clean and in good order and to wash and starch them all before festivals.

This probably sounds as if I was given all the nasty jobs, which is not true. The church had had a very difficult time during the war when a lot of the houses were empty, and now the East End was starting to live again. Our congregation on the first Sunday I was there was about six. By the time I left four years later it was well over 100. They were exciting times, building up after the war, and we all worked very hard. There was absolutely no lay leadership. The vicar trained two people to be churchwardens and in time we had a P.C.C. To start with we had to do the lot. As soon as the deacon had come Fr. Perry, the vicar, laid out a map on the floor at a staff meeting and divided it into three. We then took pastoral responsibility for our bit of the parish. Everyone who came to church was put on our Intercession list and prayed for during the week. If anyone was missing from Church on Sunday we had to know the reason by the staff meeting on Tuesday morning or we were strongly rebuked.

One morning a few weeks after my arrival Fr. Perry knocked on my door to tell me that the king was dead and that he was going over to Church to toll the bell.

It was unbelievable that this incredibly brave man, who never expected to be king, yet had inspired his people through the most terrible war in history while fighting his own illness and speech handicap, was no more. How proud he would have been of his wonderful wife who lived to be over a hundred and an inspiration to the nation.

We all kept a very strict Lent, and various cuts were made to our diet. As we were extremely well fed, this was no real hardship. Holy Week was very strict for the whole parish but very meaningful. As evening Communion was unknown in those days because fasting from midnight was thought essential, an exception was made on Maundy Thursday. On that one day in the year it was customary to fast from midday. This we duly did. After the service, which always contained the feet-washing ceremony, there was a procession, carrying the Blessed Sacrament from the main part of the Church to the Garden of Repose. This was the altar in the Lady Chapel which was covered with flowers and lighted candles, in the centre of which the Sacrament was placed. The vicar would then read Psalm 22 while staff and servers cleared the High Altar and stripped away all the hangings and furnishings, leaving the Church in total darkness. The "Garden" was the representation of the Garden of Gethsemane. Jesus in the Sacrament was alone in the garden while the rest of the world was in darkness and chaos. The disciples tried, not too successfully, to watch with him, and we now had the opportunity to do the same. A watch was kept all night until 9.00am on Friday. We left lay people to do the early hours of the watch while we returned for the only meal we would get until 3.00pm on Good Friday. It was always a simple meal of soup, bread and cheese and fruit. It then fell to our lot to cover the difficult hours in the middle of the night, and I was usually alone praying in the church for two hours at about 2 o'clock in the morning feeling perfectly safe, which says something about how things have changed. All the churches I know now only hold the Watch until midnight at the latest; often they finish much earlier, and many have given up keeping it, which I find very sad.

On Friday morning the Blessed Sacrament was brought to the High Altar. Then the big cross was brought in which had been covered since Passion Sunday. This was then ceremonially uncovered and presented to the people. It was then placed on a stool and everyone venerated it, which meant we knelt three times as we approached it and then kissed it. (The elderly and infirm knelt once and were helped up by servers.) It was very moving indeed. We then all received the Communion of the presanctified. (Good Friday and Holy Saturday were the two days in the year when there could be no Consecration of the Blessed Sacrament as the Lord had died and descended to hell.) Everything had to be consumed. After a break, when I usually went for a walk, we returned to church for the three-hour meditation. By 'we' I do not mean just the staff; everyone was expected to spend most of the three hours of Good Friday in Church. There was little else to do. There was no football, no shopping, very infrequent trains or buses—it was truly a day of mourning and fasting. How things have changed! The three of us took it in turns to conduct the three hours and I took my turn. I do not think my first effort was very good or that I did much for women's ministry, but I got through it. The second Holy Week I was there I felt very ill, and by Maundy Thursday knew I was very feverish. I carried on as usual and somehow got through the vigil and the three-hour service. (Fortunately it was not my year for taking it.) I went back at 3.00pm to enjoy our meal of fish and hot cross buns only to feel sick and faint. The vicar's wife, who was a nurse, thought something was up and sent me off to bed. In an hour or two I was covered with spots. I had chicken pox! Who did all my work on Holy Saturday I neither knew nor cared. The vicar brought me my Easter Communion and on Monday I was wrapped in a blanket and taken home for three weeks. There were now four children in the Vicarage and they all got it. The next year we all had German measles but not in Holy Week.

My first pay was £4.10s a week and £2.10s went straight back for my keep. The money for my insurance stamp was taken off, leaving me with about £1.7s.6d for everything else. It was impossible to clothe myself, save and go home every day off, which upset my mother. The fare to Wallington was about 3s.6d but at my age there were other things I wanted to do with my Thursdays off. Also, with the early start on Friday, I never wanted to be too late home. Sometimes I used to get on the underground and go to the West End or to visit friends. In the end my mother settled for me coming home about every three weeks provided I kept in touch by phone.

Strangely enough, after a second curacy in Somerset, Pam and Robert went to the parish church in Hampstead and I was able to visit them quite frequently. They had a small son and when Pam was expecting her second child I took part of my holiday to stay with her and look after them all so that she could have a home confinement. Christopher was born on Robert's day off and he had gone to the pictures. I got them to flash on the screen that the Curate had a second son!

Although I was very well looked after in the vicarage and it was quite a lot of fun all being together, I badly wanted my own space. I also thought I would be better off if I managed my own salary. Rita was by then pregnant with her fifth child and I felt I was a bit of a burden to her, partly because I was another woman. I do not think they ever really understood my reasons for moving out, but when the upstairs rooms in a house very close to the church and in my bit of the parish became available, I moved out. It had a nice big front room and kitchen behind. As the gas cooker was on the landing and the idea of having church meetings in a bed-sitter did not seem quite right in those days, I put my bed in the kitchen. One of the advantages of living in the vicarage was that it was the only house in the parish with a bathroom. My landlady had a bath with a lid on it in her scullery but I only used that a couple of times in emergencies. I usually managed to get a bath somewhere on my day off, and on Saturdays joined my parishioners at the public baths. We had many fruitful conversations queuing for our bath. My landlady was the local medium but sometimes turned up at church, and she had a heart of gold. She allowed me to have my cat and looked after it when I was away. On Sunday evenings she always invited me down to watch her television, quite a novelty in those days. She lived with her son, a quiet man who was out a lot. We got on very well and, when I left, my successor decided to go there rather than to the vicarage.

Minnie, my little black and white moggy, was more like a dog than a cat and always wanted human company. Although I knew Mrs Hall would look after her, I nearly always took her when I went home. With her wrapped in a blanket in my arms, I would take her on the bus to Liverpool Street and then on the train to Wallington, where she would lie beside me on the seat while I did my knitting. At Wallington she would go out in the garden but come immediately when I called her. I have never known another cat like her. Sadly she died aged about seven. There were not the injections and treatments for cats in those days.

We had in the parish one of those invaluable active middle-aged ladies who run the Sunday school, the brownies, the crèche for the Mothers' Union, etc. and she became a very good friend to me, especially after I moved out. She knew I wanted to learn to ride a bike and to swim, ever since my operation, and she was determined I should do both. Every evening I tried with her help to ride her bike and eventually I got my balance and rode. I rushed out and bought my first bike for £1.10s. Sadly that was stolen quite soon. My next bike cost 10s and 20p for a padlock! I rode all over London, learnt to mend punctures and thoroughly enjoyed it. My efforts to learn to swim were not so successful. I soon had the confidence to float on my back and learnt to do back stroke. Directly I turned over my heart pounded and I was gasping for breath. I now think it is the funny shape of my chest and have resigned myself to never being a swimmer! If I am shipwrecked I will float until I am picked up!

One of the things I discovered at St. Peter's was that I had quite a flare for putting together Sunday school plays, youth revues and even adult productions. We had learned a bit about religious drama at Gilmore House, and I discovered I thoroughly enjoyed putting together the readings and music, and could even write dialogue. My first effort was a twenty-scene pageant of the life of Our Lord acted by Sunday School children with music sung by the choirboys. Many of the mothers also got involved and we had a packed hall for the event, taking up a good collection for Sunday School. I later took the latter part of this pageant to create a Passion Play for adults which has been performed in many places, changing and being modernised over the years. I have also produced other playlets, both for children and adults, some written by me and some by others. Two or three have been written and produced for a whole school. Of course, some have been more successful than others, but all have had the effect of bringing a lot of people together with a common purpose and we had a lot of fun.

Just before Christmas 1954 my grandfather became ill. First he had the family cold, then it went on his chest, and finally he got pneumonia. After a few days in hospital they said he either had to come home or go into a nursing home. We struggled right through to February to keep him at home but he needed constant attention. Mother cared for him by day and Dad and I shared the night. I travelled home after work every day and spent half the night trying to do my share of the night watch. I can, and always have been able to doze in a chair and be instantly awake when needed. I have done a lot of night nursing since those days and am profoundly thankful for this gift, as it means I do get quite a lot of sleep and am not too tired next day. While he was so ill, Grandpa relived those awful days in the war, and thought I was Grandma and apologised over and over again for what he had done. It was very distressing. One day my mother felt too poorly to cope, and arranged for him to go into a nursing home. They collected him, shaved off the moustache he had had since before he was married, and within a few hours he was dead. We all felt quite guilty.

Also that winter, Sheila was ill in America. She had gone out as a student midwife to work in the hospital in Baltimore. Before starting, she had spent some time with my mother's eldest sister who lived in New York. While there she met a middle-aged couple with whom she became very friendly. They had a holiday bungalow in Keansberg in New Jersey and, realising Sheila had few friends, invited her to use the bungalow for days off and holidays. Sheila had written to say that she was suffering from anaemia and had been given a long leave to recover. We knew she was not very happy with American medicine, particularly midwifery, and was now on a surgical ward as a staff nurse. Her letters sounded rather unhappy and we were worried. Mum wanted to go and see her so I decided to give my three months notice in the parish and go out with her. We had Grandpa's estate to pay for our fare but, because of the state of the pound after the war, no one could take more than £35 out of the country. We went out together on the QE2 on the roughest crossing since she came back into Cunard service after the war. Glyn, the curate who had worked with me at St. Peter's, had also left and was working at a parish in Southampton, and he and his wife came to see us off. Mum and I are both good sailors and enjoyed the food, the attention and the fresh air, which is more than could be said of the majority. We were met at New York by Sheila and her friend Ken, and taken to the bungalow in Keansberg. Ken left next day to go back to New York and to his wife who, sadly, had Alzheimer's Disease. I was very anxious for Mum to stay with Sheila as long as possible and wanted to see Ines whilst on that side of the Atlantic. So I stayed a week, spent a couple of pounds doing a bit of sightseeing in New York, bought my bus fare to Toronto, and gave the rest of my money to Mum. My ticket home could be used on any Cunard ship going to Southampton and on any date that year! Mum stayed with Sheila for six weeks and then returned on the QE2 on her own.

10

CANADA

It was a long and rather boring bus journey up to Toronto. It took about an hour to cross the border into Canada, while everyone had their passports looked at. I later found it was far worse going the other way, although I am sure today with computer technology things have speeded up. The journey from the border to Toronto was delightful and passed through some wonderful scenery. I was met at the bus terminal by Hella, Ines' mother, who said that Ines was in hospital having had a three-month miscarriage. They already had one small son, Michael, my godson, and before I left Canada she was pregnant again and Philip George arrived soon after I left. Hella took me to her own home and I stayed there for the weekend. I was very concerned as I had deliberately left myself with only two or three American dollars, which were of rather less value in Canadian dollars.

Hella was very helpful and took me to the labour exchange but, because I would not lie and say I wanted a permanent job but could only commit myself to a maximum of six months, they were just not interested. In desperation I went to the first Anglican vicarage I could find in downtown Toronto. The Vicar was extremely helpful and told me of a divorcee who had the custody of his three young children aged 7, 5 and 3, but was forced to work during the week. He was already engaged again and needed a reliable housekeeper to be with his children from Sunday afternoon until the following Friday evening. As he was planning on marrying before the end of the year it was to be a temporary appointment. Once again God had wrought a miracle for his guinea pig! Ines picked me up every Friday evening after Mr. Gooderham and his partner arrived home. I was able to spend all Saturday with her, go to church with her on Sunday, and then after lunch she would take me back to Moore Avenue in time for Mr Gooderham to go back to work.

The children were delightful and so was their mongrel dog. I took all four out and about and, in between these excursions, I enjoyed keeping house, cooking and I believe keeping the house cleaner than it had been for years. Sometimes

Ines and baby Michael would join us on our outings and this was good as it meant we could go in her car instead of on the bus or subway. Although we had not seen each other for quite a few years, Ines and I took up where we had left off. Her English Canadian husband was delightful and so were his parents, whom I met only once or twice as they were off to holiday with relations in England. Dave was trying to make a living as a piano teacher, as well as playing in the occasional concert, but, with his young family to support and their tiny two bedroom flat quite inadequate, he was looking for something more permanent. It was possible to enjoy my stay with them each weekend and share in their plans without feeling a burden to them or outstaying my welcome, as I was not there all the time. On a few weekends Mr Gooderham was not able to come home at all and gave me extra to stay. Twice during the period of my stay he had a whole week off and so did I. On the first one I took the opportunity to go into retreat at the Anglican convent in Toronto. It was very good and I had time to appreciate my stay, spend some time thinking about what I was going to do when I returned to England and to write some poetry. I was not sure whether I wanted to go straight back into another parish. In those days one had to do a full seven years of Parish work before being considered as a deaconess, and I had done less than five. I still had a hankering for moral welfare and wondered whether to do a bit more with my nursing. There was a basic general nursing course for those who wanted to specialise in midwifery. If I did that I might be able to run my own mother and baby home. I also toyed with the idea of going into teaching as a full time R.I. teacher. I tried very hard while in the Convent to seek some guidance from God without much success. At the end of the retreat I met a girl who was also seeking guidance about her future. She was an artist and wanted to widen her experience. She was quite keen to go to Europe, and try to get a job as an *au pair* or similar, in order to find new ideas for her painting. I suggested that she tried to save up and return to England with me. I wrote Mum and asked if she would put her up for the first few days until she found her feet in England.

In the second week's holiday Sheila came up to Toronto and we went to Ottawa and stayed in the YWCA. We did all the sightseeing expected of those visiting Ottawa. I was anxious to visit the Indian part of the city where we saw some quite horrendous poverty and met some lovely friendly people. On the way back we got lost in what was obviously a French speaking area. Neither of us had sufficient French to understand directions given in that language, and as a matter of principal French Canadians will often refuse to converse in English, even when quite able to do so. We were very relieved to find an Indian who gave us good directions and we were soon back in the English part. Sheila and I were able to have a good talk and she was fairly definite that she was going to come home the following year and was thinking of nursing in the RAF. I think she was rather looking forward to being dropped by parachute with her nurse's bag and rescuing people from difficult situations. She always had a great sense of adventure and as she was double jointed could fall from heights rolled up like a ball, a trick she had perfected to Granny's horror during the old days in Berkhamsted. She would suddenly appear dangling from two floors up and when my cousins and I had assembled as an audience she would suddenly drop and get up none the worse for wear. Our week together went all too quickly and cost us a lot of money. We vowed that from then on all our pay would have to go towards saving up to get home. Actually Mr. Gooderham paid me well, as well as being very generous with the housekeeping, so I was able to save quite quickly. He also gave me all his youngest's lovely baby clothes to ship back to England for Margaret and Glyn who were living on a shoestring and were expecting twins and with whom I had promised to stay and help on my return.

My time in Canada went all too quickly. Ines' parents, themselves great sightseers, took me to Niagara Falls and Hamilton, to Concerts and to the theatre and to a variety of interesting eating places including one which was entirely 'Victoriana.' The waiters wore boaters and the place was littered with grotesque fake Victorian furniture and aspidistras. The Canadians love to imitate anything they think is historically British; for instance, they make rug chests with holes in them to look like woodworm. I found several churchyards with fake lich gates and arches, and modern graves with the tombstones put on at an angle to look ancient. As the country has no history they are jealous of our history and try hard to fake it. Actually there is a wealth of history among the Cree Indians and I wish they were more interested in that.

After five months it was time to return. I had some relations in Montreal (two cousins of my mother and their families). I stayed with one of them and they showed me round for a week and then took me to Quebec to catch the Cunard ship *Canberra* to Southhampton. I knew this cousin a bit as he had stayed with us when he had been in England with the Canadian army during the war.

The crossing to New York on the QE2 had taken five days; this journey was to take nine days. Joan also came up to Quebec and travelled back with me although we saw very little of each other on the trip, enjoying the company of our own set. I was in a cabin with three others, one lovely girl who was poorly for much of the journey and two very noisy women in their sixties who had the bottom bunks and, as they were together, they fooled around and smoked heavily most of the time. I found it best to come to bed late when they had settled down and to pretend to be asleep in the morning until they had finished their ablutions and departed. I played a lot of table tennis and some deck games and spent most of the time talking to people on deck. Being early August, it was lovely weather and very calm. The first two days we travelled up the St. Lawrence and there was plenty to see. I enjoyed the trip immensely despite my cabin mates.

Mum and Dad met us at Southampton and Joan stayed with us for only two days. She had met some young fellows on the boat and they had offered to show her England. She travelled round with them for three weeks, came back to collect some belongings and we never saw her again. She did however give me a lovely picture of the Atlantic at night as seen from New York, as a thank you for helping her get to England.

As I had some savings at home because of the limit to what I could take abroad, I spent quite a while deciding what to do. I stayed for some time with Margaret and Glyn and some time at home. I went for several interviews for teaching posts and enquired into the possibility of doing midwifery, but I really did not have enough money behind me. I went to a parish in Tottenham and nearly went there and then to several other parishes, including St. Luke's at Charlton. The more I looked the more confused I became. One day, travelling home on the No.13 bus, I heard a voice say to me very clearly, "Go to Charlton." Although I had paid my fare home I leaped off the bus at the next stop, found a telephone box, rang the rector and said I would like to come.

I was told that the church was negotiating to make a small cottage in the village available to me, but I would have to stay at the college in Blackheath until it was ready. The college in Blackheath is a training college for women ministers similar to Gilmore House, but whereas Gilmore specialised in those wishing to become parish workers and deaconesses, Blackheath specialised in those wishing to teach. It was quite fun living with the students and cycling in each day, but very bleak at Christmas when I was alone in this vast house. I was very glad when the cottage became available. It was one of a pair, which belonged to the church. The other had been done up and electricity had been put in for the verger and his daughter. Mine had gas brackets in the two living rooms for light and a very ancient gas cooker in the kitchen, but no light. My main source of light was candles. The only form of heating was a small smoky open fire in the living room. I insisted that the chimney was swept before I went in, and was promised that electricity would be put in as soon as possible, but it was not done until well after Easter. The toilet was outside and the only running water was a cold tap over the big sink in the kitchen. It was back to the public baths again. I decorated the back living room and the back bedroom, which was all I could afford to do, and bought a nice little cottage suite for the living room.

The rest of my sparse possessions had been stored at Mum's since I left De Beauvoir Town. It was a great day when the electricity was switched on and we celebrated with a house blessing and a house warming party. Pat, who had been in hospital with me when I was having all the tests before the operation, was now the almoner at our local hospital and was able to come to the party. It was good to catch up with her again. By then she had a lovely converted house at Blackheath and was able to get around quite independently.

I lived happily in the cottage for eighteen months and my successor also lived in it but, when she left, it was condemned and pulled down.

St. Luke's Charlton was an interesting parish with a lot of life. There were two curates who were both keen on acting and making a fool of themselves. We started a youth club, which we called the 'Ambassadors,' and I wrote a review, and one of the curates wrote a pantomime, which we produced for the parish. The curates lived in the rectory with the Rector and were looked after by the rector's housekeeper. I was often invited to Sunday dinner and spent my second Christmas with them, which was nice after my lonely first Christmas at Blackheath. Besides all of us, there was a Franciscan sister who worked in the parish and did a lot of the visiting. She also ran the Mothers' Union and wanted me to be an associate member, the only option for the unmarried. I refused, as I could not see the point, and said I would wait until I was a mother, which she thought very strange. I did however go to many of the meetings and was several times asked to be the speaker. Our deanery presiding member was Susan Varah and I got to know her and her husband Chad quite well. Later Chad became the founder of the 'Samaritans.' I was thoroughly enjoying myself and was quite sure I was in the right place, but did not feel I was doing anything of much use. I was also acutely aware that most of the other parish workers in the diocese of Southwark, where I was now licensed, and in London, where I had been previously, had had secular jobs before starting their training. I had gone from a very protected childhood to training and to work.

I needed some more experience of life! My short time in Canada had taught me that. As a parish worker in those days, it seemed presumed that I had taken vows of celibacy, which I certainly had not. I got on well with male colleagues and lived largely in a man's world, but working in an Anglo Catholic parish meant that any chance of meeting men romantically was quite out of the question. My spiritual director then was the Provost of Southwark, and I talked over with him how I might widen my circle of friends. One day, when walking about in the West End on a day off, I noticed a Christian dating agency and walked in. I was met with the most enormous understanding and was told that they had many people like me, and a large number of priests, on their books and would I fill up a form about my age, interests, likes and dislikes, etc. It was not primarily a marriage bureau, but a place for enlarging one's circle of friends. In a parish one has to be very careful about making close friends, so life can be quite lonely. I filled up the form in a fairly general way but said very firmly that I did not want an introduction to a divorced man. To my surprise my director, in whom I confided my actions, did not throw up his hands in horror. I think he was wise enough to know this was a very necessary part of my development in the art of human relationships. Quite soon I was sent an introduction, followed by another, and then another. All were very nice and I started getting out and about a bit on my days off. Then one of them started getting more serious than I wanted and to my horror I found he was divorced. I tried to be kind and freeze him off gently, then I got crueller, but he just would not take a hint and would turn up on my doorstep at the most inappropriate times and would not even leave when I had parishioners there.

It was getting embarrassing and out of hand. So I wrote to the agency saying please could they find someone else to befriend this chap (who had a very real need and for whom I really felt quite sorry) and to please not send me any more introductions as it was causing me so much embarrassment. My letter to the agency crossed with a letter from them saying they had given my name to a young widower who would be contacting me. I determined that no way would I meet this man! Peter's letter arrived next day asking me to meet him on Thursday evening under the clock on Waterloo station. He told me briefly that his wife had died six weeks earlier after being ill for many months and he had two young children. It was the kind of letter one just does not refuse and, as Thursday was my day off, I had no excuse not to go.

11

LOVE AND MARRIAGE

I arrived at the arranged time at Waterloo station, found the big clock and looked round. The station seemed largely deserted, the teatime crowds having dispersed and the evening trains not yet begun. Over the other side of the station I saw a man of medium height, wearing thick glasses, who was obviously giving directions to a West Indian man. I looked all round for someone else and, as it was now some ten minutes past the arranged time, began to wonder whether I had been made a fool of. Suddenly I heard a voice behind me: "Miss Adams?"

I turned to see the man I had first noticed across the station. So this was he! He told me of a cafe across the road which he knew of and invited me to join him for coffee. We ordered coffee and biscuits and cheese. I had had nothing to eat and tucked in when I noticed he had hardly eaten anything. I thought he must have already had a meal and did not learn until later that he had only picked at food since his wife's illness. We chatted for about two hours with amazing ease.

I do not ever remember talking so easily to anyone and after a while I realised I had done all the talking. As a parish worker I normally did the listening to other people's troubles and here was I pouring my heart out to a complete stranger. It was not all one way, I hasten to add. He spoke easily about his wife's painful suffering, treatment and eventual death, about his seven-year old son who had been the apple of his mother's eye and now appeared very withdrawn and confused, about his 18-month old daughter, who had hardly known her mother and had been brought up by a number of different people; about the difficulty he had had to find a suitable housekeeper with whom he felt confident to leave his children; and how in desperation he had settled for a middle-aged woman with a teenage son and daughter, an arrangement he was already beginning to regret.

When we felt that we could not stay any longer in the restaurant without eating, Peter offered to take me home. He had a very old battered Austin and going along the Old Kent Road one of the back windows suddenly fell out, scattering broken glass all over the road. Sheepishly, he pulled up and kicked the broken glass into the gutter. I felt so sorry for him: what a thing to happen when taking a girl out for the first time! To put him at his ease, when we arrived back to Charleton, I invited him in for another coffee, which he readily accepted. For company I had recently acquired a mongrel pup that was not yet house-trained. As it could do little damage to my stone kitchen floor, when I went out I put everything out of reach, put a paper by the back door and left her to her own devises. We walked through and I put the kettle on. Immediately Peter picked up the soiled papers and sat on the floor to play with the pup. It was as though he had been coming for years. We took our coffee through into the sitting room and talked for another hour or so. "Would you like to see the children?" Peter asked. I said I would and arranged to go down on the train on my next day off. He would be at work until 5.30 but suggested I went directly after lunch to spend some time with the children before he came home. He would warn the housekeeper that I was coming. It was well after midnight when Peter left and I hoped fervently that nobody in the village had seen him go.

The following Thursday I caught the train down to Orpington. I knew the journey well as for a time Pat, my almoner friend, had been in Orpington hospital for rehabilitation after she left Guy's. I went down several times to visit her and would often stop at the little general stores opposite the hospital gates to buy Pat sweets or fruit. Once I had had a cup of tea in the little tearooms there. I now noticed that the place was called Freeman's Stores. As Peter had directed, I caught the bus to Green Street Green and walked up Worlds End Lane to Ibbs Cottage. This was the right-hand one of a pair of tiny cottages. I knocked on the door and a plump middle-aged woman opened it and invited me in. She went off into the kitchen to put the kettle on, leaving me standing. I followed her through into the untidy back living room. "Get the baby if you like, she's woken up," she said. As I had no idea where the baby was, this seemed a ridiculous thing to say. Then a wail from the front room gave me a clue. I pushed open the door. The room was in total darkness so I pulled the curtains. Most of the room was taken up with a vast put-u-up, which was open and covered with clothes and bedding. (I later learned that the housekeeper's schoolboy son slept in there.) In the window was a large old-fashioned pram with a broken hood and in it a chubby little girl with matted curly blonde hair, a grimy streaked face where tears had cleansed a path through the dirt and hands that had been in the coal bucket. A certain ripe aroma left me in no doubt as to how she had spent the last few minutes. She gave me the biggest, most enchanting grin I had ever seen on a small child. I picked her up and carried her through. I asked the housekeeper for a clean nappy, a bowl of water and soap and towel. These were willingly brought but no effort was made to take the child from me. I cleaned her up, changed her and asked for some clean clothes. With considerable difficulty some were found. About four o'clock a small boy rushed in, said "Hullo," dropped his school trousers on the floor, pulled on a ragged pair of shorts which had been hanging on the back of the chair and rushed off again. It was a couple of hours before he reappeared. The housekeeper's children arrived back on the bus, and feeling slightly out of place I took the babe into the garden and played with her until her father returned.

Peter seemed surprised and delighted to see his daughter washed and in clean clothes. Cleaning Mary up was normally his first job after arriving home from work. One might ask what the housekeeper was meant to do! We all had tea together and I helped bath the children and put Mary to bed. We listened to the Archers, sitting at the half cleared dining room table, and then Peter suggested taking me home. I sensed he was feeling an intruder in his own house and wondered how he normally spent his evenings. There was no doubt that the housekeeper's family, although very pleasant, had completely taken over, and nobody had any privacy. On the way back to Charlton, Peter took me to introduce me to his sister. She lived behind the stores where I had so often called on my way to visit Pat (I must on many occasions have been served by the father-in-law I was never to know, for he had died eighteen months before.) Diana now lived alone and was trying to keep the shop going although she had been forced to give up the tearooms. Peter was very anxious for her to sell up and go to live with him and care for the children so that he could get rid of the family who had taken over his home. Like all the newly bereaved, he was finding it hard to think rationally. When we got back to Charlton we talked again for a long time. I heard no more for about a week, and was quite busy in the parish and with our revue. In the end I telephoned to hear that they had all been ill and the car had broken down; however, Peter was hoping to see me on my next evening off if he could get the car started. I had written briefly to my parents, telling them that I had met someone with two children and we were getting on very well, and that I was hoping he would come over to Wallington to meet them and to take me back after my day off. He arrived in the end, having been working on the car all evening, and after several calls to report on progress. When my parents saw the state of the car I think they wished their daughter was going back by train!

Our relationship progressed, the housekeeper proved a complete failure, they closed the shop and Diana moved in to look after Roger and Mary. As many Thursdays as possible I went down to look after Mary and give Diana a break. The summer holidays came and we all stayed at Wallington. Around this time Sheila came back from the States and was at home and looking for an entrance into the Princess Mary Royal Air Force nursing corps, which was later to take her to Swindon Hospital. She and Peter got on very well and played tennis together while I looked after the children. My mother took to Roger in a big way, and seemed to understand him, and he seemed very fond of her. Poor Peter was put under the spotlight, and my Father criticised him for many things, his dress, his behaviour etc., but we expected that. My mother was naturally very concerned that I should not let my sympathy for this sad bereaved little family rule my head. I had no intention of doing so. It was for me quite incredible that I had met someone who was interested in all that made me tick and yet treated me as a perfectly normal human being and had no intention of making any allowances for my past medical history. I could not play tennis with him so he played with Sheila in such a way that I could enjoy what they were doing and never felt jealous. If I had to sum Peter up in one word, it would be *honest*, not always kind, not always tactful, not always understanding, but always *honest*. One of our sons has inherited much of this honest quality and I admire it although it isn't always easy to live with, as it can at times be quite hurtful. At that time it was the honesty which attracted me, and in a way gave me an anchor. I tried very hard to hear God's voice in all this and shared with Peter my deep faith. He was desperately seeking an anchor and a new direction for his life. As a plastics technologist he knew that the local job he had was not secure although the firm had been very good to him during Lee's illness and he felt he owed them loyalty. His pay was appalling and I knew he could do better. He was on day release to study further and do his City and Guilds qualification: after that there was hope that he might land a better job. We went to church together when possible and prayed together for guidance for us both.

The holidays over, we went back to the old arrangement with me going to Green Street Green for most of my days off, and Peter came over at weekends, sometimes bringing the children. In October he asked me to marry him. It was the day before a big parish party and my family was coming to it, so we told the rector and the parish were told at the party. It was already becoming difficult to keep the secret, and if it had not been for the Enrolling Member of the Mothers' Union giving us cover, it would have been impossible. I don't think many were surprised, and the children were a bonus as far as they were concerned. I went to bed full of love and champagne. At 10 o'clock next morning Peter arrived looking very gloomy. He had not slept and was feeling very guilty thinking about Lee, his first wife, all night and wasn't at all sure he wanted to get married after all. We talked, we prayed, we drank endless cups of coffee and late in the afternoon went into Woolwich to buy a ring. I was never in any doubt that Lee would always be a part of our relationship and had no difficulty with this; in fact, I encouraged him to talk about her all he wished.

When he put photos away I got them out again. Although I knew he would often give anything to have her back, he could not, so it did not need to affect our relationship. (The only day I ever felt jealous of her was on the day Peter died and was reunited with her. The feeling soon passed.) I do not think either of us doubted that it was God's will for us to get married. We prayed a lot together and took the children to church, and my entire parish took him to their hearts. After the Christmas services we went to Wallington until New Year.

Since losing her parents Diana had had a few quite serious epileptic fits. Often these would occur at night and always came on with little warning. One day Roger found her under the dining room table and, being terrified, had gone out to play without telling anyone. Peter was furious with him but I felt it was quite understandable so soon after losing his mother.

On New Year's Eve Diana was playing cards with Sheila and our parents and Peter and I were in the kitchen when dad came out to say that Diana had suddenly thrown her cards in the air and was having a fit. Sheila was looking after her. Peter was extremely worried. We had planned on being married in June and I had given my notice to the Parish to leave after Easter. This would be well after the first anniversary of Lee's death. Now Peter wanted to bring the wedding forward. As I had no intention of having a big wedding in Lent, it meant the last Saturday in February. We spent the rest of the weekend writing to Lee's family trying to explain the reason for our extreme haste and the next day I went back to attempt to make my peace with the rector and the bishop. The rector could not have been nicer, nor could my colleagues. They were only concerned that I stay long enough to be the Wicked Fairy in the pantomime Sleeping Beauty. The Bishop, however, was a different story. He made me feel I was letting down the whole of the Church of England by getting married at all. I cannot remember whether he was celibate himself, but he would certainly have liked it for all his ministers. Three weeks later I left and took Mary to my parents to prepare for my wedding. My parents wanted a big do, with top hat and tails, and Dad had already written to the Admiralty to ask permission to wear his dress uniform. I felt this was rather unfair to Peter and very unfair to Lee's family. After some discussion we decided to give my parents their head, as they were paying. There was no time to argue. I had bought the material for my dress and for the bridesmaids' dresses while still in London and, as soon as I got home, spent days on end sewing with Mary sitting on the floor beside me playing with the bits. I decided to have a train long enough for Roger to carry as a pageboy, and he had a wonderful time going to Moss Bros. with his father for his suit and top hat. The three big bridesmaids wore dresses of bubbly nylon; Sheila's in turquoise, Diana in gold, and my young cousin (also Diana) in pink. Mary's little dress was off cuts from mine. We were still turning up hems the night before the wedding. Never has a bride been so unprepared. We decided to have a nuptial mass at 10.30 so that we could fast from midnight (no evening Communions in those days) and to be married at Beddington church, which I attended when in Wallington. The provost of Southwark, my director, married us and preached, the vicar of Beddington celebrated and Fr Bear, my old rector, said the prayers and assisted. One of my curate colleagues was an usher.

I was very concerned how Peter was really going to feel on our wedding day so soon after losing Lee. I think he realised how desperately I was trying to please my parents who were both such efficient planners and went along with their wishes for my sake. We also wanted it to be a day to remember for the children. It had to be their day too. I insisted that Peter should plan our week's honeymoon on his own. He took Roger into his confidence, telling him where we were going, and giving him the trust to keep it a secret from me. At the reception he gave Diana an emergency phone number, as she and the children were to stay with my parents for the week, and told me we were catching the three o'clock train at Paddington. The wedding car took us to East Croydon underground.

12

THE GUINEA-PIG MAKES HISTORY

Our destination was Paddington to catch the 3:00pm train to Penzance, fondly known in those days as the "Honeymoon Express" because of the large number of newlywed couples who used it every Saturday. Certainly we started our journey with just one other embarrassed, confetti-covered couple in our carriage. Further along the line we picked up a couple who must have been in their seventies. It was hard not to be very aware of the other couples as, in those days the average compartment held just six people although, on long distance trains, a corridor linked these with access to toilets, restaurants, etc. Passengers sat three a side facing each other. We arrived at Penzance in the dark and found our hotel. Dear Peter had booked a double room but had not told them it was a honeymoon. His face when he saw the twin beds was something I shall never forget. He tipped the porter and rushed away to find the manager. The outcome was that we ended up with the best suite in the hotel, which we certainly had not paid for. It provided us with a good story for friends when we returned.

Peter was insistent that I should not unpack, as we were not staying. A car had been arranged to pick us up at 6:00am on Monday morning and take us to Land's End Airport. By 9:00am we were at our destination on St. Mary's (the largest of the Scilly Isles). Most of the week was spent exploring St. Mary's and Tresco and visiting the more remote islands. I have wanted to return there all my life and was able to do so just a few years ago. Many things are the same but large pleasure boats run between the islands and there are proper jetties and landing stages. I missed the rowing boats that landed you on the beach and the thrill of wondering whether the boatman would return for you at the arranged time! It was a wonderful week and I am very glad it was a surprise. In our absence my mother and our sisters had done their best to make the cottage at Green-Street-Green as welcoming as possible, and, on the following Monday, Peter returned to work and I began my new career as wife and mother. I felt very proud as I pushed Mary in her pushchair into Orpington to do my first shop.

We were not to stay in Orpington long. We knew that Peter had the offer of a new job in Essex and fairly quickly found a large five-bedroomed house in South Woodford. The cottage and shop were both sold and, with the help of a sympathetic bank manager and my father, we moved in. Peter worked hard and, by spending every possible moment on the house, converted two of the bedrooms into an almost self-contained flat, where a young couple soon took up residence. He then turned his hand to converting the enormous dining room into a bed-sitter, which a Greek couple was delighted with. They could speak little English but were an instant hit with the children. Both couples were invaluable when later I became pregnant and my heart did funny things with very little warning. Despite the rents paying the mortgage, money was still very tight. Mary had had such a poor start in life, that I was very anxious to be with her as much as possible, so arranged to "daily mind" one or two other children. This worked very well and gave Mary company. One of the attractions of the house was that there was a very good little school just up the road for Roger. We visited the church at the end of the road and found we did not fit at all. At the time it seemed of prime importance to find a church where we would all be happy and the children would be cherished. We found this in St. Peter-in-the-Forest, a walk of about a mile and a half, largely through Epping Forest. We went as a family to every service we could and, before long, Peter was editing the Parish magazine and had trained as Group Scout Master. I was Baloo in the Wolf cub pack, Roger a cub, and the boys as a kind of mascot adopted Mary, as she appeared at every meeting in her pushchair.

Sadly, despite all our joy and hope for the future, Peter's bad patch began to catch up with him soon after we were married. He seemed so happy with his job, with his scouting and with his children, and yet there were often times when something quite trivial would spark off the most terrible black moods. I knew he was missing Lee still, and that I could never replace her, but I loved him dearly and felt this was my personal sacrifice of love. His doctor referred him to the Maudesley Hospital and he was put on a drug to which he soon became addicted. He was on it for many years, and the time when he was finally weaned off it for his health's sake was another very black and depressing time for him.

To make life even more difficult for Peter, Roger did not settle at school and after several threatened miscarriages, the baby I was carrying, and which had quickened six weeks previously, suddenly stopped moving and was pronounced dead at six and a half month's gestation. My gynaecologist was too frightened to give me an abortion which would have needed a general anaesthetic, and advised that I continue for a while and see what happened. The experience of knowing you are carrying a corpse within your own body was most unpleasant and had a bad affect on us both. When I finally did go into labour at church one Sunday morning I was not expecting it. My sister in law had come the previous evening and I had made a rabbit pie with lots of onions. When I awoke that Sunday morning, I thought this was the reason my tummy felt peculiar. During the service, the discomfort turned to pain and I asked Peter for the car keys so that I might go and sit in the car. He was on sideman's duty that morning and it seemed an age before the rest of the family appeared. By this time I was in full labour. Once home, he called an ambulance and arranged for the girl in the upstairs flat to follow the ambulance in his car so that he could come with me. The thought of strange ambulance drivers playing midwife was more than I could bear. With hooter blaring we bumped along the cobbles of the Mile End Road, and at some point picked up a real midwife. I just made it to A and E at Guy's Hospital. I have always wished I had asked whether it was a boy or a girl and will never really know, although I always think of him as a boy. We had called him Martin since the beginning.

As I had carried him alive and dead for seven and a half months, I was terrified I would be put into the maternity ward and have to see all the happy new mothers with their babes. Kindly, the doctors decided to do their calculations from the week when they knew he was dead, and when, under normal circumstances, I would have been aborted, and I was sent to the gynaecological ward for a few days and then allowed home. Doctors, nurses, family and friends bombarded me on all sides suggesting what I should do next. Some advised me to start again as soon as possible and produced convincing arguments why I should do so. Others said I had a ready-made family and I should be happy with that. It is true I loved Roger and Mary dearly and the four of us were a happy family unit. My father had recently paid for Roger to go to a boarding school, which catered for his good brain far better than the local school. For a couple of years he was very happy there and learnt to play the piano very well, playing entirely by ear. Both he and Mary developed great musical gifts and excellent business sense, which I am sure they have inherited from their half Jewish mother.

Looking back on my behaviour today, I fear I must have appeared to many people as very selfish. God had given me a loving husband and two children, all of whom were badly damaged by the sickness of the person who for so long had been the centre of their lives. I longed to help them, and gave them all I could, but the dominating force in my life was to prove to the world that this person, who had been the first to survive open-heart surgery, should also be the first to give birth naturally. Lord Brock was enthusiastic that I try again as soon as possible, but my GP was a little apprehensive, fearing that Lord Brock wanted to use me as a guinea pig. I think this was the first time the term guinea pig was used of me. However, I very soon became pregnant again and, despite several threatened miscarriages and periods of angina, during which I had to take to my bed, made it to seven months.

It is a known fact that people with heart trouble have very small babies, so it was very important that the baby should not be born before its time. People reading all this today, when all babies are screened regularly, will find much of this strange. X-rays were available, but were only used in the most extreme circumstances, where the mother's life was at risk, as it would almost certainly damage the foetus. I was admitted to Guy's Hospital at thirty-two weeks and put on strict bed rest. An attempt was made to send me home for Christmas, but I was re-admitted after a few hours. It was very hard on all the family. My parents were wonderful and had everyone to their house for Christmas, and, as I said before, all our lodgers turned up trumps. Early on the morning of January 7th 1959, after fourteen hours of labour, and just ten years after my surgery, surrounded by some twenty or thirty doctors and medical students, I gave birth naturally to a healthy baby girl—and so together, Margaret Clare and I made history!

13

MARGARET CLARE

My first thoughts as my little daughter lay in my arms was that she was just like a little fledgling bird, her breath coming shallow and fast. Perfectly proportioned, she was the size of the china doll I had had as a child. Most of the babies I had seen in the past seemed to have heads that were too large for their bodies, whereas Clare, as we called her, had a small head and chubby little limbs. To me she was *perfect*.

"Is she all right?" I asked.

The midwife took her from me, weighed her, and said she seemed fine but would have to go into the "Prem" nursery as she only weighed four lbs. fourteen ozs. She was hustled away and I suffered the indignity of being stitched up in front of my huge audience. Late in the evening Clare was brought to the ward for me to have a peep. She was wrapped in so many blankets all I could see was her tiny red face. It was three days before I saw her again! It was customary on the ward for mothers to stay in bed for a week and then they were allowed to get up and taught how to change and bath their babies. It was presumed that all mothers would feed their babies unless there was good reason for not doing so, and regularly every four hours the babies were brought into the ward for twenty minutes' feeding time.

When all had been returned to the nursery, aluminium dishes with lids were brought to each mother so that, if they had any milk left, this could be expressed for the milk bank. This was used to feed the small babies who needed extra bottle feeds and those who needed feeding during the night. Everyone hated expressing as it was seen as painful and difficult self-torture, and, as I was not yet allowed to feed my daughter, it was expected that I would produce the most milk for the 'Bank'. The sarcastic remarks of some of the nurses when they saw my feeble efforts only made the agony of my separation from Clare worse and I became very low. It's true that Peter was allowed to dress up in gown and mask each evening and see her before visiting me. He told me she was not in an incubator but in a little cot at the side of the nursery and described every detail about her that he could. All the other mums in the ward seemed very young and I, at thirty, felt like a granny. Most of them smoked and pop music blared all day. The only other mother approximating my age was a woman who, I noticed, was bottle-feeding her baby, holding him at arm's length to do so.

I never saw her cuddle him or hold him close and was determined to get into conversation with her, difficult as it was across the ward. My early experience of moral welfare work made me wonder if the babe was up for adoption. Sadly I never got a chance for a proper conversation with this lady and have often wondered about her. All I knew was that for three days I had not seen Clare and was devastated, while this woman did not want her baby. On the second night I was given him to feed and cuddle and even had thoughts of going home with 'twins'.

Ward Sister, who had been off duty for several days, came back, and on doing the rounds after visiting time, found me in tears. She was furious that no one had brought Clare for me to see and marched into the nursery and fetched her wrapped up in blankets and sat with me while I fed her. For the first time I began to know the joys of motherhood. The next morning I was taken into the 'Prem' nursery in a wheelchair, covered with a sterile gown and wearing a mask, to feed her again. I promptly passed out with the heat so we were back to square one, but I did see her twice a day from then on. As soon as I was allowed up, Clare was thought strong enough to go into the ordinary nursery, although still not allowed into the ward. I looked after her in the nursery until we went home, but always wearing mask and gown.

We went home when she was fifteen days old and just five lbs.! As I had so desperately hoped, Clare's safe arrival seemed to bring healing and peace all round. Besides being a major event in Guy's Hospital, everyone was relieved and excited. For my parents she was a first grandchild, born of the child they never expected to live. Peter was ecstatic and his health began to improve. Roger, home from boarding school for Christmas, was delighted with his new sister and Mary, who I feared might have her nose put out of joint, happily joined me in the role of motherhood, bathing and feeding a very lifelike baby doll given her on Clare's birthday by our Greek friends. Even Lee's mother and sister seemed delighted and, from then on, regarded her as much one of their family as Roger and Mary.

Like Hannah in the temple, I felt that such a miraculous and wonderful gift from God should be dedicated and given back to him as soon as possible. I, therefore, arranged the christening before leaving hospital and sent out invitations with the birth announcements.

Two weeks before the great day, rushing back from church on Ash Wednesday, I collapsed with paroxysmal tachycardia by a busy road junction and crossroads. There was a lot of traffic about but, because it was just at the traffic lights, no one noticed a woman sitting by a pram desperately holding on to a child lest she ran too close to the traffic. There was an enormous water works on the corner, and finally, in desperation, I tried sending Mary into the building for help. I knew she was remarkably sensible for a four year-old but feared she might be too frightened to leave me. I was to discover how sensible she was. Within minutes, two men arrived to say an ambulance was on its way. A man in an *Evening News* van appeared and, with the aid of sweeties, persuaded Mary to leave me and allow him to take her home. I prayed that our Greek friend would be there for her. The ambulance arrived and Clare and I were taken off to Whipp's Cross hospital.

I was given drugs to steady my heart and Clare was brought to me every four hours for a feed. We were home in a couple of days but for the next eighteen years, despite regular drugs, these attacks of paroxysmal tachycardia were to be a regular feature of my life. I lived a perfectly normal life and even learnt to drive and often the gap between attacks would be several months. The pain was terrible, as my heart raced to about three times its normal rate and I was usually sick. All the children learned at a very early age not to panic, to leave me on the floor and to fetch a bowl! If it happened in the street someone always coped and I usually went into hospital for 24 hours. If it happened at home the family left me and continued looking after each other until I recovered.

My drugs were changed from time to time but it made little difference. Sometimes I could postpone an attack by pressing on my jugular vein, but the attack always came in the end. I also learned a great deal about the Church's Ministry of Healing and was regularly given Anointing and Laying on of hands by my spiritual director. Our great worry was that I might have an attack while looking after very young children, so Peter and I prayed for their safety and, although I was never "healed" in the sense that I still had the attacks, God took care of our children, and the older ones learnt how to cope with the situation. God always seemed to be in charge.

On March 1st Margaret Clare was christened. My sister Sheila and Peter's cousin Eileen were her godmothers and my cousin Richard her godfather. The service was immediately after the morning Eucharist at St. Peter-in-the-Forest. After the Baptism the Priest carried her up the aisle and laid her on the altar to dedicate her to God. I have never seen it done before or since and have never done it myself. I have often wondered if it was because she was such a miracle baby.

When Clare was four months old Peter lost his job and we could not pay our mortgage. We lived on social security, the rents from the flats and the little I could earn looking after another couple of four-year-olds as company for Mary. It was costing us a great deal trying to keep Roger at boarding school and he seemed happy although he did come home for the Easter holidays with two broken arms, having been pushed over the banisters. We were afraid he might be being bullied but his reports were good and we were very anxious to do the best for him whatever it cost. We put the house on the market and it sold very quickly to people willing to take on our tenants. Peter, meanwhile, found a good job which necessitated being away from home during most of each week, travelling round the country and to the continent. It was working for a Continental firm of plastics technologists who made plastic cartons for drinks and sealed packets for many food manufacturers and medical suppliers. We therefore decided it would be better for us to move into a cheaper house not too far from my parents in Wallington, Surrey. They had a large house and had converted the upper floors into several flats. We were able to take one of the flats temporarily while we house hunted. Within three months we had found and bought a house in South Croydon where we were to live for the next four years. As soon as we were settled, it seemed a good idea to try for a second child while I was still not too old, and I soon became pregnant. We liked our local church, St. Augustine's, and I became the group leader of the young wives and Peter was on the P.C.C. We also became very friendly with the Reader and his wife who had two daughters between Mary and Clare in age. Their house needed a lot doing to it, and so did ours, so every Saturday saw Margaret and me looking after the children in one house while the men worked in peace on the other. We let one of the rooms to an unmarried mother who had kidney trouble and sudden attacks of great pain, so we were able to help one another and it was company when Peter was away.

In October, just as things began to look rosy again, our lives were once more to be devastated!

14

TRAGEDY

It was October 1959 and our cup of happiness knew no bounds. We had found a lovely house in Croydon, very near a church where we felt very at home. Roger was happy at boarding school, Mary (now five) had settled at her first school, Clare was now 9 months and thriving and I was pregnant again. To celebrate such happiness Peter and I decided to spend an evening walking in Keston Park and having a snack at the local pub. Blissfully happy, we returned late and went to bed. After what seemed a few minutes, but was in fact several hours, we woke to the shrilling of the telephone. Grumbling, Peter pulled on his dressing gown and went down to answer it and I went back to sleep. He returned later with two cups of tea and crawled into bed beside me. With tears running down his face he broke the news. It had been my father on the phone. My beloved sister Sheila had been killed on the road at the same time as we had been out celebrating!

My way of dealing with any tragedy is to become very practical and to be very 'in control.' Within an hour the children had been assigned to our faithful lodger and we were at our parents' house to hear the full story. Sheila was then a ward sister in the Princess Mary Hospital. She had recently acquired a little open topped car, which was the joy of her life. Only a couple of weeks before she had been to Croydon to see us and our last sight of her had been of her going down the road, with the roof down, waving enthusiastically. Apparently, not soon after this, she had gone over a ditch and done something to the suspension, which she intended to get fixed as soon as possible. On that fateful day, she was due to go out with another sister, but at the last minute, the other girl's boyfriend had turned up. In a rash moment, she decided to take two of the convalescent airmen on her ward for a spin in the car to celebrate one of their birthdays. Both men had been in the hospital for about eighteen months with TB and it seemed such an innocent jaunt. Nobody ever found out exactly what happened except that, turning a corner, the car must have turned right over, throwing her out on her head and she must have died instantly. The two men were found by a passing car wandering up the road and very shocked and taken back to the hospital. The Sunday papers had a field day and my poor father was faced not only with the necessity of identifying his smashed up daughter, but also of knowing that, had Sheila lived, she would have faced very strong disciplinary proceedings from the RAF. As it happened the whole incident was played down at the inquest for the sakes of my parents and the two young airmen.

I was extremely worried about my mother. She had always suffered from never seeing Colin at peace after his death and I was determined history should not repeat itself. My father's cousin was the funeral director and I arranged with him to bring Sheila home for a day or two before the funeral. Peter and I cleared out the little study and I bought some tall candles and borrowed some stands from the church. We had our own little chapel of rest. Despite some bruising round her neck, Sheila looked far better than I dared hope. It was wonderful on the day of the funeral, as the little room filled up with wreaths and flowers from the RAF and from both sides of the Atlantic, to hear Mother say to each visitor as they arrived, "Come and see my Sheila asleep." I really do believe that this saved her from a severe breakdown.

There is always so little time between the death of a loved one and the funeral, especially in cases of unexpected death, that often very wrong decisions are made. The days when the loved one was laid out and kept at home until the funeral will never come again, but I do believe that the few people who have the courage to insist on having their loved ones home for a while do derive enormous strength and courage from it and it gives them the ability to say goodbye at the funeral. We are not a very pretty sight when we arrive in the world blue, bloodstained and wrinkled, but to those we love we are perfection itself, drawing out feelings of love as nothing else can. We are actually a much prettier sight in death as our features change and our skin becomes smooth, soft and tranquil, whatever the suffering that has gone before. There has to be time to say goodbye in whatever way is most appropriate. The love has to be surrendered, an endearment expressed and tears shed, and this can never happen satisfactorily in a quick visit to the funeral directors. I believe now that this is very important where children are involved. I remember quite early on in my ministry going to the house where a four-year-old child had died of leukaemia. The little girl was laid out in her bedroom with all her toys round her and her siblings took me in to see her as though it was the most natural thing in the world. They were a wonderful family and the funeral a joyous occasion where we could all, through our tears, give thanks for the little life. I have never forgotten it.

After Sheila's funeral my own pain caught up with me. I lost the baby I was carrying and when I thought I was coping really well I would suddenly find myself crying or, worse still, trying to cope with frequent attacks of my old enemy tachycardia. At the time of Sheila's death, Peter and I agonized over how to tell Roger at boarding school. We rang the headmaster who knew about his mother's death and explained that it was essential that Roger was given the news as tactfully as possible and given the opportunity to grieve, as he was devoted to his aunt. I am sure they did their best but it was a great shock to him. After careful thought we decided it was best not to try to get him home for the funeral, a mistake which we were bitterly to regret. From that moment his attitude to his school changed and his work, from being very promising, became diabolical. It was eventually decided by all parties concerned, including a child psychiatrist, that he should come home and go to a local school. Sadly, things with him were never to be the same again and, although our relationship continued to be reasonably good, I do not feel that I was ever much good at helping him sort out his life. I suffer great pain over our relationship to this day, but that is another story.

Thirteen months after Sheila's death I gave birth to a son. His birth was very different from Clare's. Once again I was taken into hospital for several weeks before the birth but when it happened it was most unexpected. My waters broke in the middle of ward prayers and he arrived on the trolley on the way to the delivery room. First reaction seemed to be that he had died from the shock but he was resuscitated although remained very poorly. I haemorrhaged and, because of my racing heart, they were fearful of giving me a transfusion. All night long both our lives hung in the balance. Twenty-four hours later we were both in the ward and I was to discover how much things had changed in the ward in less than two years. The babies stayed in the ward all day, even at visiting time. One never saw nurses or anyone else in a gown and seldom in a mask. There was no more expressing; the prems were fed on Carnation milk (later condemned as being quite unsuitable for babies). I know that Julian was tube fed at night, which prevented him losing too much weight, and ten days later we went home. Both the girls had had measles and were being cared for by my mother while I was in hospital. Mary was better and allowed home to go back to school provided she kept away from the baby. Clare had to stay with my mother for another two weeks and I missed her dreadfully. I struggled to feed Julian but he started to lose weight and I had to supplement with Carnation. Two good things came out of this very difficult time. Because I was so tied to the house with my fragile baby and frequent attacks of tachycardia we lashed out £5 and bought a second-hand television. We also found out what a lot of very good neighbours we had. One of these was June Brown (alias Dot Cotton of "Eastenders" fame) who, in those days, lived directly opposite us. Her eldest child Louise was the same age as Clare and they had played in their playpens together since they were a year old. Her younger daughter Sophie was about six months old when Julian was born. June came over frequently, nagged me into making greater effort to feed Julian myself and always understood how depressed I was feeling. Although the character of Dot is obviously very overdrawn, June was the same big-hearted straight-speaking person who would do anything for her friends and would always see the best in anyone. I do not know in those early weeks, after I came out of hospital, how I would have managed without her. At that time her husband Bob Arnold was Jack Warner's sidekick in "Dixon of Dock Green" and June herself went from time to time to take part in local productions of Shakespeare and the odd television play. As time went by she would often ask me to have her girls when her agent called her. I was also able to have the girls for her when she sadly lost her first son. I was then able to return a bit of the love she had shown me.

By the time he was six months old Julian was starting to thrive. Once on solid food he became quite a little pig and quickly made up for his bad start. I started taking in other children again, which I enjoyed immensely. The only problem was once *again* Peter's health. He was in bed for some weeks with what was diagnosed as diverticulitis, but looking back now I fear it could well have been the start of his cancer. When he was better he was away with his firm for days on end and frequently made trips to the Continent so my life revolved more and more round the children and the Young Wives. The Vicar and his wife were very supportive and even took Clare and Julian, while other friends had Roger and Mary and Peter and I could go away for a weekend together.

15

THE FAMILY GROWS

One day the social worker, who had approved me as a 'daily minder', asked me if we would like to become foster parents and take two small children permanently. The younger baby, then five months, had had enteritis and her development was about that of a two-month-old. The little boy, Mark, was aged about twenty months. Their mother was a widow, whose husband had been a racing driver and been killed before Jane was born. She was now being evicted from her flat and, as she was a nurse, was trying to get the children cared for so that she could take up a residential position. There was no problem about Mark but there was a serious legal problem, which made it difficult for me to take Jane. The law at that time said that one could not foster a child under school age who was within nine months of the age of one's own children, presumably so that one's own child would not be neglected. The fact that many people had twins seemed to be quite overlooked. The social worker was particularly anxious that I had Jane because of all my experience of rearing very small babies, and took the whole matter before a court to have an exception made, and we waited.

Unfortunately the children were brought to us just three days before we were all going on holiday to my mother's flat at Littlehampton. My Aunt Eileen and cousin Richard were also joining us there. The holiday was a complete nightmare. Peter resented the children taking up so much of my time and was grumpy. Roger cashed in on the situation and delighted in winding up his father. The babies were very unsettled in their new surroundings. Jane took ages to take her bottle and was suspicious of my handling. I was torn in every conceivable direction and had little confidence in my ability to cope if my heart decided to go into overdrive. If it had not been for my aunt I could never have coped, although the guilt of knowing we were ruining her holiday added to the strain. My aunt and cousin were due to stay on for another week after we went home, and then be joined by my other aunt, Vida, and her husband. When she suggested that I leave Julian with them for the week so that I could settle Mark and Jane and give some time to the rest of the family, I gladly agreed. Both my aunts devoted themselves to him, taking him long walks in his pram and playing with him and he came home a much happier little boy.

Looking back on this period of my life I realise how stupid I was. Most people, I now believe, would have been thankful to have enough health to enjoy a happy marriage and four lovely children, and maybe I should not have agreed to having Mark and Jane, and should certainly have said we would not contemplate having them until we had had our holiday. It was part of a pattern that has been with me for so much of my life. I just cannot say "no" and have spent so much time trying to keep an impossible number of balls in the air. I now believe it is not from fear of denying others but from fear of denying myself the satisfaction of trying to be superhuman. It is as though that very strong willpower that brought the guinea pig back from the dead just will not let up on her. My efforts to be "normal" have resulted in making me to a large extent abnormal. Now in my twilight years I wonder if something inside me has always been saying "If you say no you will die." I now do not mind saying "no" nearly as much, and will mean it, but then I have had my "threescore years and ten" and am now in bonus time.

The rest of our four years at Croydon were good years. Peter enjoyed his job more and more and I was able to adjust the children's routine with the help of many good neighbours and friends, so that when he came home I had time to be with him and listen to his adventures. I had an enormous second-hand pram and decided to have a second hood put on it so that I could go out with a baby at either end, the shopping in the well and Mark, who was hopeless on reins, slung across the middle. Then, with Clare on reins, I frequently pushed the children to South Croydon station and travelled to Wallington in the guard's van to spend a day with my parents. This super pram was to come in useful again when my sister-in-law, Diana, had twins.

I adored my grandmother who was then well on in her nineties and living with my mother. I wanted to spend as much time with her as possible as her life was fading. She died peacefully, her half-finished library book still open on her lap. To me she represented 'Peace'. She suffered much all her life but never criticised others. I believe she always saw the best in everyone. She was not a great churchgoer but her prayer life was the very fabric of her being. Often she fell asleep on her knees by her bed and my mother had to wake her and get her into bed. Although one of the old school, and living all her life in her 'widows weeds' she always tried very hard to understand new things and to learn about the world of her grandchildren. She was blessed with remarkable eyesight and read a great deal. She was a very gracious lady indeed.

Mark and Jane thrived and we soon got used to having four children under three as well as Mary who was a very bright seven-year-old. Fortunately the school was only round the corner so she was able to go to and fro with her little friends each day. I also started daily minding again and, despite her poor start, Jane seemed to be developing well as she tried to compete with Julian and the others of her age. She was very slow talking but well able to make her needs known. Otherwise she caught up very quickly and was soon running around.

Soon after the drama of Julian's birth, and when I was back to normal, Peter confided in me that he missed all the things he had done in Woodford, with the scouts and the magazine editing, and was wondering what he could do for God and the church, which was possible with his strange working commitments. He was usually at home on Sunday to help me take the children to church and would often look after the babies and cook lunch so that the older children and I could go to Sunday School which followed on the parish Communion service. But apart from Sunday there seemed little he could do for the Church. We prayed about this and wondered whether God might be calling us to get involved with the branch of Samaritans, which was being set up in Croydon. Up until this time the Samaritans had operated only at St Stephen's in London. Now Chad Varah wanted to start setting up centres in other towns, and one of the first of these was to be in Croydon. I had known Chad's wife Susan through Mothers' Union when she was my Deanery Presiding Member in London. She was by this time the head of the Overseas Department. We decided we would at least attend Chad's training sessions and see what came out of it. It also gave us an excuse to have a baby-sitter and go out together. To cut a long story short, Peter ended up a supervisor and I was the rota organiser, something I could do from home. By working around Peter's work schedule I was able to keep him feeling useful and made many new friends on the phone through trying to keep the rota covered. Sometimes we were able to get away and do a night duty together. Anne, Mark and Jane's mother lost her first post and the next one did not require her to be completely residential. We offered her the two rooms at the top of the house so that she could have her children when she was not at work, and this gave me more free time. In return she would look after our children while we were on Samaritan duty. On the whole it was a happy arrangement.

However, once again this happy time was to be short lived. There had been talk for some time of Peter's firm closing down its branch in England and the inevitable finally happened when he came home to tell me he had three months' notice. At first three months seemed quite a long time and we did little about finding him another job. Also he was away more than ever at first packing up the firm in various places. Further attempts to find a similar job seemed very difficult and I realised that Peter's depression was becoming very acute. He seemed to be losing heart in the plastics industry, which was becoming very competitive.

My parents were also going through a bad patch. At 60 Dad had taken early retirement from the Bank of England. He had a bank pension, but it was to be five years before he could get his main pension and, much to everyone's surprise, he announced one day that he had got himself a job caring for the most mentally disturbed children in the secure unit at Carshalton Hospital. The work was very stressful and he was to do three months on duty and then have three months off, during which time he could claim unemployment benefit. He did this for several years and was apparently very good at it, but I found it difficult to visualise my father feeding, changing, washing and playing with these very handicapped children. I admired him enormously. He said he just wanted to do some nursing for Sheila, and we all realised how much he still missed her. My mother went through all Sheila's possessions on her own. Dad came to me one day and told me that he believed she had discovered something about Sheila's time in the States that was very distressing, but she would not tell him what it was. It seemed she was refusing to talk to him about Sheila anymore. This he found very upsetting and their marriage was, we knew, going through a very bad patch. Many years later, after my mother died, I discovered that Sheila had had a baby before we went out to visit her and had presumably had it adopted. That was why she had spent all those months in New Jersey, and it was from that that she had been recovering when we went to visit her. I still hope one day to trace my nephew.

Now Dad was approaching 65 but was still physically strong and young at heart. I knew he could not continue at the hospital after retirement age but needed a challenge and so did my mother. Otherwise they would get on each other's nerves. One day, during Peter's last weeks at work, he said to me as he left the house, "If you have any time today, think and pray for the right solution to know what we all should do and, if you come up with any ideas, ring me."

By lunchtime I believed I had the answer. *We would buy a hotel.* My parents would have the right expertise to run the financial side which was not our forte. Peter would enjoy being host and I would do the bookings. It would be an interesting environment for the children as they grew up, and I could visualise a very good family business. I rang Peter and then my parents. To my surprise everyone was struck with the idea. By the weekend both houses were on the market and we were driving round looking for hotels.

16

HOTEL LIFE

The first decision that had to be made was where to look for a hotel. The seaside seemed obvious, but where? Mary had done very well at school and had won a scholarship to the Girls Public Day School trust in Croydon. As my school in South Hampstead had been G.P.D.S.T., it had always been my dearest wish that any daughter of mine should go to a Trust school which for girls was at that time the best in the country. We were all so delighted when Mary made the grade and she had started to settle there. The last thing we wanted to do was to uproot her, but it seemed that we had no alternative. There was a G.P.D.S.T. school in Portsmouth, and one in Brighton, so we would try and buy a hotel in one of these towns in the hope she could transfer. We realised this would only be possible if there was a vacancy, but hoped for the best.

Leaving the children with friends, Mum and Dad, Peter and I spent several long days looking at hotels in both towns and finally short-listed three, one in Brighton and two in Southsea. We spent a whole evening discussing the merits of the three places and it was obvious we were not going to agree. Diplomatically we then held a secret ballot, writing our first choice down. As there were four of us we were bound to come up with a winner. Fortunately Mother and Peter decided on the Alhambra Hotel in Southsea.

The hotel needed a lot doing to it, but there was potential. We put in a low offer, which was accepted. We got the impression that the owner wanted out but did not want to make any effort to get out. Solicitors became involved and a date was agreed for the move. When we finally arrived with the contents of our Croydon home and quite a few large pieces of furniture from my parents' home, we found the previous owner still there, still with nowhere to go, and with no chance of our getting into the owner's flat. We had to sleep for several weeks in a big family guest room. Fortunately it was November, so there was plenty of time before the season, but we were anxious to hold a launch weekend for family and friends and to be open for Christmas. There were schools to sort out and two of the children had birthdays in the first week of our arrival. Fortunately most of the staff had agreed to stay on, largely, I think, because they fell in love with the children. Thanks to them we achieved all our targets. We had a very successful launch over two weekends and were thus able to give family and friend a choice.

By Christmas we were in full swing and were able to do a full four day Christmas complete with all the trimmings, children's party, and outing to the pantomime for the princely sum of £26. This is now the rate for one night's bed and breakfast, but in those days (1963) that was £1–10s a night. We were able to employ an elderly chef (his cooking was much better than his temper), and a waitress. My cousin and his girl friend also came to help and proved themselves invaluable. Dad was in charge of the cellar and Mum of the children and the accounts at which she was meticulous. Peter was the perfect host and my main job seemed to be arranging the bookings and striving to get the right people into the right rooms.

As the season approached and we started to get rather full it was obvious that we could not have three members of staff, the family and my parents all living in and still have enough rooms to let. The first summer the whole family lived and slept in one room. My parents still had a big house to sort out and sell in Wallington and they decided to go for a few weeks and get things moving. We, meanwhile, would look for a place near at hand where they would be comfortable. I was lucky in very quickly finding them a ground floor flat with big rooms and a large garden. The whole house belonged to an old sea commander (like Dad) and his wife, and they preferred to live in the top of the house where they could see the sea and not be responsible for the garden. When Mum and Dad came up to see it they were thrilled and the two couples quickly became firm friends. With some of the money my parents made from selling the house in Wallington, they were able to buy the house adjoining the hotel, which gave us a lot more scope. We now had a complete flat of our own and the children had their own living room and space away from the business. Also, we were now able to take a whole coach party and still have a few rooms available for passing trade. In the winter we filled the place with students and my cousin coped while we had a holiday in October. My parents came in and out, and Mum kept a firm eye on the accounts. In all, life was very good and the children thrived on hotel life.

School-wise, things were not so good. Despite all our efforts we could not get Mary into the G.P.D.S.T. school and paid for her to go to a private school. This had a nursery attached and Julian went with her. Clare, then five, started at the little Church infant school along the front where later Julian joined her. As a family we all settled at St. Margaret's, Eastney, where the children were made very welcome and Peter was soon on the P.C.C. I was able to keep my hand in, helping with confirmation preparations, with Mothers' Union, where I soon became deanery and then Diocesan Overseas Chairman. At one time I was training all the Sunday School teachers in the Diocese and they had great fun coming to the hotel each week. We became very friendly with the Vicar and his wife. They had two lads at university who came and worked for us in the holidays. Their daughter was the same age as Mary and they were friends for years. Three years later we were in for another surprise.

17

SURPRISE, SURPRISE—MARTIN CHARLES

Early in 1966 we realised that I was once again pregnant and that my father had Alzheimer's disease. We weren't at all sure at first that we wanted the baby as the hotel was going so well and it was hard to see how we could manage if I had to spend a long time in hospital. I was nearly forty. Also Peter was very frightened, as I had been so very ill after having Julian. He wanted me to have an abortion, which I would never have agreed to even if it cost me my marriage. I did, however, agree to go and see Lord Brock who had always kept an eye on me since my operation, and the obstetrician who had delivered Julian. I shall always remember my long lonely train journey to Guy's. How hard I prayed that the doctors would be on my side and encourage Peter that all would be well. I first saw the obstetrician who seemed to lean heavily towards the abortion idea so, by the time I saw Lord Brock, my heart was in my boots. I was beginning to realise with each passing moment how desperately I wanted this baby and could not wait to see him. Lord Brock read the obstetrician's notes and his recommendations and said, "Don't worry, old thing (his usual term of endearment for his patients), it will do you far more harm to have an anaesthetic for an abortion than to have a normal delivery. Go home, rest all you can and plan for your baby." The journey home was nearly as worrying as the journey there as I still had to tell Peter. I need not have worried. God had gone before me and I found Peter relaxed, calm and I sensed he was looking forward to a baby as much as I was. As it turned out it was the most wonderful blessing either of us could imagine and was to bring us closer than ever.

During Lent I worked hard with the drama group at Church planning and producing a Passion play which I had produced many years ago in Hackney, and which was based on the famous Poplar Passion play which in turn took much from Oberammergau. Everyone worked very hard up to and including the dress rehearsal on the Tuesday of Holy Week. The production was to go out on the Wednesday and on Good Friday.

That night I started to haemorrhage. Now we were both looking forward to the baby, and had told the other children, who were equally excited, it looked as though we were going to lose it after all. I was rushed into our local hospital and, by the next morning, the bleeding had stopped, although the doctor was certain I had miscarried. I was told to get up and walk about and see what happened. Nothing! I walked round the ward worrying about the play and our Easter guests. Still nothing happened, but I was not allowed to go home. I needed a D. and C. (a small operation to scrape my womb) but nobody wanted to risk giving me an anaesthetic because of what Lord Brock had written on my notes. I sat in hospital all over Easter and practically the whole of the cast of the play came to tell me how things had gone in my absence. Who needs a producer when the cast knows what they are doing! As far as I could make out, both nights were a sell out and the only minor tragedy was that Caiaphas went on stage without removing his spectacles!

I feared that the following week I would be sent up to Guy's. Instead, another heart specialist came from Southampton to see me and, after doing various tests, decided I was fit enough to have the anaesthetic. He would, however, be in the theatre just in case. My operation was arranged to be last on the list the following Friday. The day arrived and I was forbidden any food or drink from 6:00pm the previous evening. Various people came to see me during the course of the day, the heart specialist, the obstetrician, and the usual endless procession of students and junior doctors. All listened and commented on the state of my heart, and no one put a hand in the area of my tummy until the anaesthetist came. He felt my tummy, jumped back and asked me how many weeks I was. Finally he said, "This is one of the best fourteen week pregnancies I have felt for a long time. I think you should go home." I asked: "Can I have something to eat?" I believe in getting my priorities right! He left to tell the other doctors of his findings, giving my order in at the kitchen on the way. At five o'clock, the time scheduled for my operation, I was on the phone to Peter to come and get me. He did not at first seem too pleased. I later learned that believing I would be safely in hospital for the weekend, he had decided to decorate our sitting room as a surprise for me, and was at that moment stripping the wallpaper off the walls. I went home and sat on a chair in the middle of the room watching him work! My obstetrician remained mystified and believed I had been expecting twins, and, very rarely, it had been known to lose one and for the other to survive. As my sister-in-law had four-year-old twins, this was possible. The heart people believed that because I still had a hole in my heart, oxygen had leaked back to the placenta and kept the baby breathing. I prefer to think of it as a miracle, as I knew from the very first that this child was a very special gift from God.

I threw myself into the coming hotel season and was remarkably well. Our regular guests and the staff were almost as excited as the family at the thought of the patter of tiny feet. Mary, who had always had a problem with an ankle, had an operation. Two weeks after coming out of hospital on crutches, the whole area went septic and she had to return to hospital for a bone graft. Then one day at the height of the season Sue, who looked after the younger children and had had them out on the beach, came in to say that Julian had gone very funny and been very sick and she had had a job getting him home. He looked dreadful, so I put him to bed and called the doctor who looked at him and went away to get a paediatrician. By the time the paediatrician arrived Julian was unconscious. Meningitis was suspected and an ambulance was sent for. At the very time the evening meal was being served in the hotel I was being driven away in an ambulance with my unconscious six year-old in my arms. At the hospital they did all the tests and Peter closed the bar early that night and came to take me home. We rang the hospital several times during the night and were told there was no change. In the morning there was still no change although I think he knew we were there. The following morning he was sitting up eating toast and doing a jigsaw. Such is the resilience of the young. After a week in hospital he had made a complete recovery.

Meanwhile my parents had moved. Mrs Spiers had died and Commander Spiers sold the house so Mummy had found a large property once again, and was busy buying furniture to fit out an upstairs flat that she could let. My father was quite uncommunicative and seemed unaware of much that was going on around him. Once again I had to go into hospital several weeks before the birth which was due in the second week of October. Arrangements had to be made for the children. Mary was twelve and we thought she was old enough to survive with Peter and the staff in the hotel. Some very old friends from Croydon days offered to have Clare. Geoff was Julian's godfather and they had looked after Mary on several occasions in the past as they had two girls between the ages of Mary and Clare. My mother then felt she could cope with one despite having to do everything for Daddy. The trouble was that Mum or Peter brought Julian into see me frequently, and Mary could come in with her father, but poor Clare could only speak to me on the phone so felt abandoned. I know everyone did their best to give her a good time and she went frequently to play with her great friend Louise

Arnold but at four one can feel very misunderstood and I think she still feels that I had abandoned her.

Five days before expected I went into labour and was taken to the delivery room where I remained for the five days going in and out of labour. By the day I was due to deliver I was very tired, Peter was exhausted, and the doctor and midwives were fed up. At lunchtime a decision was made to break my waters. The next four hours Peter and I did crosswords between contractions and at six o'clock Martin Charles arrived quietly, with no fuss, and with just a midwife in attendance. This was the fifth of Peter's children but was the first he had seen born, and he was ecstatic. It seemed to create a special bond between them which was to last for the next eight years. I never remember Peter getting angry with Martin who always seemed to be the peacemaker in the family, and still is. One day I discovered, in a cathedral, a card saying that the name Martin means someone with "moral strength and a positive outlook"—who "shows lasting qualities of love and leadership; and is a steady ship in a stormy sea." Martin had and still has all these qualities. He was certainly well named. Strangely enough, Clare and Julian are equally well named. Clare is "bright, shining clear." She is "perfection, ladylike and caring, blessed with many feminine virtues, someone to treasure and a shining light." Julian is "masterful; promotes activity and makes difficult decisions. A man who loves adventure and is prepared to take a chance in life; an individualist." I never realised until then how aptly we had named our children.

After ten days in a nursing home Martin and I returned to the hotel. During my stay in hospital I had become very friendly with the other mum—in her thirties—a naval wife who was expecting twins who it was thought may have been Siamese. In the end she was delivered of a very large boy and a very small girl. Both babies thrived on Carnation milk, which I attributed to Julian's eventual progress. I do not know what either of us would have done without it. Two years later it was banned and every tin had to carry a warning: "Not for infant feeding." Up to that time it was the mainstay for many premature and underweight babies. Such is fashion!

Martin thrived, being looked after by all and sundry in the hotel. At six months old he would sit in his high chair outside the hotel dining room with his food in front of him and any passing waitress, sometimes his mother, would put in a spoonful. Then he would be positioned by the sink to play with the teaspoons while the washing up took place. Everyone adored him, his siblings, the staff and guests alike. He seemed to enjoy everyone's attention and was a contented child.

My father, meanwhile, was becoming less and less able to do anything for himself. Mummy struggled to keep him socialising by pushing him out in a wheelchair, but he was a heavy man and it all became too much for her. In the 1960s there was not a lot of help for carers and so she kept him amused by putting on all the sports programmes on T.V. This did more than anything to keep him quiet and happy. After the season we had him in the hotel for a week and looked after him while Mum got away for a few days. One evening he was sitting by the fire in our sitting room while Peter and I had a bit of late supper. I asked Peter who was playing a certain football team in the Cup Final. Suddenly a voice, which for two years had only said "Yes and No" and usually yes when he really meant no, and no when he meant yes, said very distinctly: "Nottingham Forest!" I have never ceased to wonder at Alzheimer's. It seems that when the brain loses everything else, one or two things are never forgotten. A pianist will never forget how to play, a knitter will continue to produce beautiful knitting and a gardener will keep gardening with success. The brain is a very mysterious organ. Finally Dad got too heavy and helpless for Mum to manage and, after a brief spell in hospital where they tried in vain to get him to walk, he was sent to a nursing home where he died at the young age of sixty-nine.

My mother wanted to be buried with my sister and brother, so she sent Dad off to be buried with his parents in Southgate Cemetery. Having looked after him for as long as possible, she seemed to close that chapter of her life and threw herself once again into the housing business which had always been her first love.

By 1971, my cousin had left us, our reliable old chef had left, and new staff came and went. One day we decided the children were beginning to suffer and it was not worth wearing ourselves out any longer. We decided to put the hotel on the market at a fairly high price, telling ourselves that if we got a good offer we would sell, and if not we would try and struggle on for a few more years. As luck would have it we did get a good price and had to move fairly quickly.

18

PASTURES NEW

Having run a hotel for nine years, and now with four children still at home, we found it hard to think what we should do next. About eighteen months before leaving the hotel, Peter announced to me one evening that he had lost his faith and would no longer pray with me or go to church. He said he had been feeling like this for some time but had put off telling me, as he feared he might damage my faith. I assured him that that was impossible but I was worried about the children. Our faith had always been a family thing and he had encouraged both the girls when they were having confirmation instruction. He had been behind me all the way when I trained some eighty budding Sunday School teachers who came to the hotel on winter evenings. He often witnessed in a very strong way to visitors during late night chats in the bar. I was, to put it mildly, dumbfounded. For the rest of our time in Southsea the children continued to go to St Margaret's with me where Clare and Julian were in the choir. The vicar's youngsters were all going through the rebellious stage and so was Mary. Feeling I was to blame for this bomb which had hit the family, I rushed to see my director. Arguing with Peter was quite futile and, at the time, he seemed to have all the answers. He had a scientific mind and had obviously been exploring new theories and going down intellectual paths which I could not hope to understand. The blessed Trinity, Father, Son and Holy Spirit were all as real to me as the members of my family; I did not always understand, but love kept us bound together. Denial of either was an impossibility. I think Peter had been wrestling with the knowledge that I had something he badly wanted and had not yet found and was secretly rather envious. My biggest cross was that we could no longer pray together, especially after we had had a bad day. All our married life, when we had had a disagreement, it was not just a case of 'kiss and make up', but rather kiss, make up and pray together. As I have said, Peter suffered with his nerves and the time we were quiet together with our Lord was balm to us both. Something very real and important was missing from our marriage. I was very lonely in many ways, especially as we had now to make momentous decisions about our future.

Peter's family had always had a shop and he liked the idea of one day owning one himself. We found a shop in Drayton High Road, and as there was a supermarket fairly near, we decided to specialise in delicatessen. We cured our own ham and had a wide variety of cheeses. It was all rather fun. The flat over the shop was far too small for our large family, so we let it to pay the lease and the overheads, and spent the rest of the money from the hotel on a large chalet style house in half an acre of ground in beautiful Oaklands Grove, Cowplain. At the end of our road were fields, and oak woods, excellent for the dogs and for the children to play. Had we gone to the Town Hall and made some enquiries, we might have found out that plans were already in to build an enormous council estate, complete with shops, infant school and pub. The value of all the 'Des. Res.' in Oaklands Grove was to plummet. Six months after our arrival the bulldozers moved in!

Mary had by now left school. There was some talk about her going on to do music and my mother had my father's piano brought over to encourage her. Although she had quite a talent for music, she was now courting and was anxious to earn. She soon found a job in an insurance office and did very well. Phillip had been one of our students in the hotel and he and Mary had been friends on and off for quite a while. He came from a large family and Mary got on well with them all. Soon after our arrival in Cowplain, Mary had her eighteenth birthday, a wonderful excuse for a family get-together and for friends and family to see our new home. Meanwhile, Clare and Julian had started at Cowplain Secondary School. Until the previous September this had been an all boys school, but Clare was now in the first group of girls. The school was to change dramatically during their time there, more than doubling in size, and changing from Secondary Modern to Comprehensive. It became very impersonal, and after Clare left at sixteen, Julian found life there very difficult. I found it almost impossible to find anyone with whom I could speak with as a parent.

The shop, at first, seemed to be going quite well. We expected it to take time to build up the required goodwill and both of us worked very hard. We were there together in the mornings; at lunch time I held the fort while Peter took out the deliveries, and soon after he came back I had to go home to meet the children from school, later returning to fetch him home. As we had only one car it often required quite a juggling act.

I had at last learnt to drive, about two years before we left the hotel. I say at last as I had been trying for years, several times failing for such stupid little things as forgetting to take off the hand brake. When at last an examiner said he was failing me not for anything I had actually done wrong, but because I was far too nervous to be let loose on the road, I was tempted to cut my losses and give up. Then I met a chap who had spent the whole of the war teaching young teenagers to fly Spitfires, and was now specialising in nervous drivers for whom coping with nerves could be a life and death situation. He took me out and said I had all the makings of a good driver if I could only have confidence in my own ability. He concentrated on the things I did right and ignored the things I could have done better. I soon had my little pink ticket. My test was in the morning and in the afternoon Peter, fearful that I might lose my new confidence, volunteered to look after the children while I drove to Godalming, had a cup of tea with my aunt and then drove home again. I never looked back and have now been enjoying driving for nearly thirty-four years.

One of our ventures when we had settled at Cowplain was to sell our Cortina Estate (bought with hotel shopping in mind) and to buy a VW Dormobile and a little Elf for me to run the children around in. We had some good holidays in the Dormobile and in the summer let it out, and managed with the Elf. The profit on this was good but the season very short. It did however pay for our holidays, and we bought an extension canopy and blow-up beds so that two of the older children could camp outside.

Sadly, it soon became evident that the shop was never going to pay, despite being allowed to open Sunday mornings, which the supermarket could not, but the number of articles we were allowed to sell kept us in permanent fear of breaking the law and I was very unhappy with the situation. We were losing money very fast and I left the shop for Peter to run with part-time help and returned to what I was best at, looking after children. Social Services renewed my licence to care for children on a daily basis and suggested I might like to run a council nursery in my house and garden. First I would have to find approved help, as the law required that there should be three of us, as at no time should the children be left with fewer than two in charge. Amazingly enough, this paid remarkably well, as the council paid all monies straight into our bank account and I just drew out the money needed for the staff salaries. Every morning saw me starting out at 7.30 to pick up most of the children in the Dormobile. All the children were under school age including some tiny babies. There were no seat belts and only a couple of child seats in the car; the older children hung on to the little ones and carrycots were slung across the seats. Looking back, I am appalled at the risks I took. One morning like that today and I would be up in court, but at that time no one turned a hair. With my able assistants we got the nursery running well and the children were fed well and seemed very happy. Most of the children were collected by their parents in the evening although one or two had to be run home. The immediate financial pressure off, Peter could look round unhurried to find a suitable buyer for the shop, and then to find another job.

Mary was planning to get married and fortunately we had put sufficient money aside when we sold the hotel. Phil was round after work most days and was wonderful with the children, giving them piggy-backs round the garden and keeping them amused until they were collected. Sometimes he would run them home. Little did I know how much I was to come to rely on him in the next two years.

19

NOTHING LASTS FOREVER

Peter's new job was to take him to the telephone exchange. It was not wildly well paid but with my contribution from the nursery we could manage. The men at the exchange were expected to do unsocial hours, which meant that he worked from five o'clock to eleven o'clock most evenings and all night at least once a week. Also, he did Sundays which I loathed, although it did mean we had Mondays completely free. It also meant he had to sleep during the day after a night off and did not want to be disturbed in the morning. After about a year it became apparent that to have a horde of small children arriving in the house at 7.30 each morning was definitely not on. That was the end of my council nursery, and, as soon as Martin was old enough to start school I would have to look for another job. It was around this time that I seriously started trying to breed dogs. We had the room in our garden to have kennels built and the little playhouse I had bought for the nursery made an excellent puppy-rearing house. After losing our Peke we had, while still at the hotel, acquired a Cavalier King Charles Spaniel and had her mated. She decided to give birth in an armchair in our flat while we were enjoying a family lunch in the hotel to celebrate Clare's confirmation that morning. There were only two puppies and one later proved to be deaf, although his wonderful owners taught him to respond to hand signals. I then acquired a Ruby Cavalier bitch and, with the two of them, we did quite well. Peter always preferred Pekes and missed his little friend who had spent most of her life in the hotel bar with him. I then discovered when we got to Cowplain that a Peke breeder lived up the road from us. We became great friends and I bought two bitches from her. We were in business. Clare has inherited my great love for animals and shared her room and often her bed with the dogs. When I closed the nursery I discovered that one family were emigrating to Australia, and were preparing to have a beautiful Labrador cross destroyed. They were, of course, delighted when I offered to take her on. Kim settled very quickly and bonded particularly well with Julian who started doing obedience with her. She was quite the best-behaved dog we have ever owned and won many rosettes and competitions for her young handler. Her only fault was that she tended to lag when walking to heel and this I am sure was the only thing that kept her from qualifying for Crufts. Labradors just do not seem to be able to wrap themselves round their handler's leg like a Border Collie or German Shepherd does. My Cavalier and Peke pups sold well and I also reared and trained a magnificent young Cavalier stud dog. I was often asked to go and whelp the bitches he had sired, for which I charged the enormous sum of £15. It seems ridiculous today for hours of work and sleepless nights. However, one could buy a really good puppy then for £25. Every whelping I have ever been privileged to be part of (which by now must be well over 100) has taught me so much about the wonder of creation. Every puppy is so perfect from its tiny ears to its little claws. Then that first cry when the pup's little face turns from grey to pink. Sometimes I have had to work for a long time to stimulate the little one into life, and in this the mother will help me by licking and then by pushing the pup away so that she can call it back to her. Together we get the pup going. I know what to do because I have read books and been shown by more experienced breeders. The bitch knows because for her it is natural. Mother instinct, we call it, and it is wonderful indeed. Sometimes a pup does not make it and will die in a day or two despite great efforts on my behalf. The bitch knows instinctively if a pup should be left to die and will push it into a corner and turn her back on it. All my efforts to persuade her otherwise are of no avail. She instinctively knows best. For her death is not a tragedy but a fact of life. How wise she is. She does not wrestle with the theology of natural selection, which has always worried this guinea pig; nor has she read Our Lord's words about the two men in the field or the two women at the well when one is taken and the other left. She just understands that some of her babies are meant to die and she accepts it. I often wish that we who believe we are made in God's image had the grace to accept it. How much my dogs have taught me.

My next venture was to get work in a factory, which made parts for television. I worked on the bench to start with but was not quick enough to keep up with the more experienced staff and after two or three other jobs ended up soldering panels. This was piecework and I loved it. The quicker and more accurate I became the more money I made. Also, because the right wires had to be soldered in the right places it used my brain as well as my manual dexterity. The hours 8—12am fitted in with the family, although I had to rely on Mary to get the little ones off to school. She was excellent with Martin and they all knew Peter was there even if in bed and asleep.

In September 1973 Mary and Phil were married at Waterlooville. Our friend Harry Gilroy came from Eastney to conduct the service. Clare and Phil's sister Barbara were bridesmaids and Martin and Phil's little nephew Mark were pages. I made all the dresses and I shall always remember Peter proudly leading his elder daughter down the aisle. He looked so well and happy. Once more life was good, but it was not to last.

Washing up at the kitchen sink one morning I had a vision. I saw myself walking down the aisle of a church between my two boys and we were following a coffin. I went cold. Was I really seeing what I thought I was seeing? It was something I could not share with another soul, not even my spiritual director. I had had visions and premonitions before but never anything like this. It was so vivid. I looked round and saw all our families gathered, but there was one strange omission—my mother. I felt relieved. Strangely, I do not believe I could have born it if she had been. It took me some days to recover from this extraordinary vision and I tried to convince myself it was all in my imagination but, somehow, I knew it was not.

In the summer of 1974 Peter's cousin Eileen (Clare's godmother) and her two young children came from New York to stay with us. All went well until one evening when the younger children were in bed and I had just fetched Julian and Kim from a training class. I decided to go down and meet Peter from work. I had allowed myself plenty of time and was driving slowly down Portsdown Hill....

I woke in hospital with a doctor and a policeman leaning over me. No, I had not been drinking. Why was I here? Why had I no feeling in my arm or leg? At that moment Peter walked in. How did he know I was here? I had foolishly committed the worst sin of driving slowly when very tired, had fallen asleep at the wheel, gone across the road and straight into a lamp-post. A car coming up the road had caught the back of me, making the impact even more severe. I had broken my pelvis, my right arm in three places, and had a great gash across the back of my head. I was extremely lucky to be alive. I was taken to the ward, my right arm plastered from my shoulder to the tips of my fingers and my legs in traction, and for two weeks could barely move. Two days after the accident, a policeman arrived at the hospital to serve me with a notice for dangerous driving. He had been to the house and was quite amazed to find I was in hospital, and even more at the extent of my injuries. Apparently, after the crash, I had got out of the car, walked to the ambulance, told the police where I was going and where my husband could be found. I had also given, on request, my home address—all this while completely unconscious. Apparently I had been in the hospital quite a while before I came out of my coma. It makes one realise how wonderful the brain is at storing knowledge at the back of the mind, although I find as I get older it becomes harder and harder to bring it to the front. I was in hospital nearly a month and not allowed home until I could walk reasonably well with sticks. It was several more weeks before I was out of pain and fully mobile. Dear Eileen was wonderful, looking after my children as well as her own while I was in hospital. What a way to spend a holiday.

The case went to court and I was fined for driving without due attention. It so happened that on the day of the accident I was not driving my car, which was in the garage for some minor repair, and, as the Dormobile was out on a let, Peter had borrowed a little car from a workmate. The car was uninsured and should never have been lent to us. Fortunately for us the judge was far more upset by the other man's lack of insurance, so my sin was judged very leniently, and we ended up with a very small fine.

Once more the guinea pig had survived. Soon after this Peter started complaining of stomach pain. He had had several attacks of diverticulitis and the doctor did tests for kidney stone and put him on a strict diet, which was to contain no dairy products. He got steadily worse and the treatment swung to that for gastric ulcers and almost overnight his diet was changed from a "no dairy products" one to an almost all milk diet. His illness, the doctor believed, could well have been brought about by the shock of my accident. We jogged along. I lost my job at the factory and because of Peter's condition felt unable to do anything too permanent. I would have a go at giving Tupperware parties. I joined, was encouraged by a very helpful leader, and contacted everyone I could think of who might let me have a party in their house. It could be fitted in to the needs of the family and gave me the confidence to get driving again. However, Peter's health was declining, the older children getting rather out of control and, in the midst of everything else, Mary and Phil announced their intention of emigrating to Canada! After a rather miserable Christmas I went one night to meet Peter from work. He usually liked to drive home but on this night asked me to drive. We dropped off his friend and then he started to cry. He sobbed like a baby that he could not stand the pain, that he could not go to work anymore, and that he just did not know what was to become of us. He never went to the telephone exchange again and next morning I drove him to the doctor.

There was at this time a consultants' strike going on and it was very difficult for any GP to refer anyone to the experts, so I in no way blame our doctor for continuing to try to get to the bottom of Peter's mystery illness. "Do you think it might be cancer?" I asked one day. In those days the word was taboo and I was told, "Don't be ridiculous." I knew Peter had very firmly in his mind the fact that his first wife had died of the big C at the tender age of thirty-two and we both needed more reassurance. He spent most of each day in bed and the rest of the time sitting in his chair watching television. I knew he was in a lot of pain, felt sick all the time and eating was a great struggle. He complained very little but was miserable, short tempered with the children, and despite the reassurances of the doctor was very frightened. One night it all came to a head. I had to call the doctor in the evening and she agreed with me that he needed to go into hospital. Her dilemma was getting him in during the strike. The only emergency ward she could think of was the renal ward. "I know his problem is not renal," she said to me, "but Because of the pain he is in I am going to plead ignorance and get him in. Once he is in their care they will not send him home." In the morning the ambulance arrived and took him in. For nine hours he laid on a stretcher in outpatients, uncomfortable, vomiting and in pain, while they X-rayed him (at last) and finally sent him to the ward. As I had to get back to the children Mary and Phil came from work to stay with him until they had found him a bed. The next day, while I was visiting, a senior surgeon came and told us he had a massive tumour in the bowel which must be removed as soon as possible. It was no shock to us, nor did we believe him when he said it might be benign. We were just so glad that at last something was being done. The operation took place on Monday. When I arrived at the hospital Peter was barely conscious. The ward doctor took me into sister's office and told me that the surgeon had removed as much of the tumour as he could but that the cancer had spread into his stomach and with further treatment we could look to another two or three years if we were lucky. It was just no surprise. My brain went quickly into overdrive wondering what to say to the children, how I was going to cope, and why I was feeling so angry when I needed to be calm. I was sure about one thing: for as long as he lived Peter was going to come first and we were going to enjoy every moment we had left. I sat by Peter's bed. He opened his eyes and said, "Well, is it or isn't it?" I could not lie to him "Yes, love, it is!" I said. We did not know then that we only had five precious months.

20

MY ANNUS HORIBILIS

Peter was in hospital for another two weeks, most of it spent in isolation as he picked up a very unpleasant smelly infection in the wound. We were told that directly this had cleared up he could go home but would have to return to hospital for a course of radiotherapy. He did not have a great deal of faith in this because of Lee's experience, but took it in his stride. Once home we lived as normal a life as possible. We went out with the family, visited friends and made plans. I returned to doing Tupperware parties and Peter started going out in the car. He was eating fairly well and did not seem too bad.

I think it was around this time that we first realised how God had blessed us in giving us Martin. He seemed to understand Peter's mood swings, and was patient and forgiving, as only the very young can be. Clare and Julian found it very hard and spent as much time as they could away from the house. It was Martin who watched television with Peter, made him cups of tea, and fetched and carried. I do not know how we would have coped without him. All of them were helpful with the dogs and, at one point during this time we had around seven dogs and several puppies awaiting sale. Thus we jollied along. Peter's firm had to pay his basic salary for six months and we dare not think any further. The day Peter went into hospital again I took Martin to be with my mother while I drove him in. I was a little worried about her, as she had had a bad cough. She was always a great cigarette smoker and I had noticed that, with this cough, she had cut down considerably on the number she smoked. That evening, when I went to collect Martin, she said she did not feel she could have him again and that the doctor had arranged for her to have an X-ray. She had kindly avoided telling me all this before, because she did not want to give me further worry. It was not many days before I realised that I had a husband with presumably terminal stomach cancer and a mother with lung cancer. I have never felt so alone. It was a nightmare.

His radium therapy over, Peter came home again, feeling worse than ever. Mother went into hospital and, after a few further X-rays, the doctor told me there was no point in operating or giving her any form of treatment, other than painkillers, and that at her age the tumour would be slow growing and she could live quite a reasonable life for quite a long time. My main worry with her was that she lived alone in her basement flat, although the caretaker of the block was quite a good friend and did spend more and more time with Mum as she became weaker. Often I drove Peter to be with her while I was out and about. Their illness gave them a bond in common and they were both telly-addicts. It also made Peter feel useful which was good for him. At the end of February Peter was back in hospital and we were in debt in a big way as by now his salary had been reduced to half. The only thing I could think of doing was to sell our big house in Cowplain and try to find us something smaller. I found a little house in Cosham, which had a bit of garden for the dogs and three small bedrooms. It was a doll's house compared with what we had had but, on Peter's birthday on March 4th, I took him from hospital to look at it, and we agreed to give it a go. He came out of hospital again just before we moved and spent two days looking after Mother while Phil hired a van and, under his capable leadership, the boys and several friends moved us. We were there just six months; I never finished unpacking and in that time all our lives were to be changed forever.

During Peter's third hospital visit the doctor told us that his case had been refereed to a lady specialist who was researching a new form of cancer treatment called Chemotherapy and would Peter be willing to be used to help in research? Why was this guinea pig not surprised? Peter was only too willing to try anything. We were told he would have to have a series of fortnightly injections and, on the day before each injection, he would need to have a blood test. We were warned that the treatment would be painful and that he would feel very poorly after each injection, then would feel better gradually, deteriorating as the next injection became due. If, at any time, either of us felt we had had enough, the treatment would stop. Before he was discharged he was given the first injection. The lady specialist who gave the treatment was very austere and refused to have any conversation with me. All the hospital staff seemed in awe of her. We called his treatment his Red Indian treatment because of the coloured band he had to wear round his head, presumably to avoid as much hair loss as possible.

Visiting Mum one day I found her in tears and quite desperate. I knew I had to look after her better, so promised to come the next day and take her home. The only way to cope was to turn poor Clare out of her room, and let her sleep on the sofa in the living room. Only much later did I realise how the poor girl suffered. She was sixteen, just starting in the world of work, and it must have appeared to her that I did not care what she was up to as I was so wrapped up in sickness. I know she had several unhappy relationships during these weeks and a mother who was unapproachable, and not even her own room to escape to. Also, Julian was running wild at school and doing very little work. One day they both came home saying they felt ill. Two days later they both had chickenpox! Peter went for his blood test and was refused his chemotherapy because he had shingles. It meant Mother had to be got out of the house that day before she too got shingles. She was already far less mobile than Peter and it would have been extremely serious for her to catch it. I telephoned my cousin Richard on the Isle of White and asked if he could come over and help me find a nursing home where Mummy could go until the crisis was over. We found one before the end of the day and Richard took her in. It was an extremely good place and I think she was as happy there as she could have been anywhere. Three weeks later the chicken pox was a thing of the past, but Peter still had not had his chemotherapy. He now had a big patch of shingles on his back and the cancer was slowly spreading up his oesophagus and eating was impossible. At last the specialist spoke with me. "I just don't know what to do," she said. "If I give him his injection, the shingles will spread right round and kill him. If I do not give it, the Cancer will spread and he will starve to death." She had tears in her eyes and I realised suddenly why she would not speak to me before. The emotional strain on any doctor, who is ploughing a lone medical furrow in a so far uncharted field, must at times be unbearable. Whatever the results the courage and unselfishness of all doctors striving to make new discoveries, and knowing how high the risks of failure are, leave me with enormous admiration! For my part I had been used as a guinea pig so successfully in one particular field of medicine and, now that Peter was being used in another, I expected the same miraculous results, and found it extraordinarily difficult to come to terms with this setback.

Peter was taken back into hospital for the last time. He did not want to go, nor did he want anyone other than me to nurse him. My sister-in-law agreed to come and stay and look after things so that I could stay at the hospital. I slept in an armchair by his bed and was told to help myself to anything I wanted in the nurses' kitchen. No one could have been better treated. Our new vicar in Cosham came to visit and spent some time talking to me, said a prayer, and left. Peter accused me of sending for him and trying to manipulate him, which I certainly would never have dreamt of doing. On the Sunday Phil came and announced that he was going to stay with Peter so that Mary and I could go to the hospital chapel. During the week we spent in the hospital two things impressed themselves on my memory. We spent a lot of time watching a little television, as it was the Wimbledon fortnight. Peter had always wanted Arthur

Ashe to win. That year he did. We had always been West Ham supporters. That year they had won the F A cup. It was a strange time. My other memory of this hospital week was Peter's almost frantic desire to be some use to someone after his death. The doctor told him kindly but firmly that no one would want any part of his diseased body and all he could leave were the corneas of his eyes. I think that was his lowest moment. Next morning we were told he could go home or stay as he wished. I rang the council and said that if I was to nurse him at home I needed a ripple bed, a commode and a pulley erected over the bed so that he could help me lift him. By the time we went home in the afternoon all had been delivered and installed. District nurses were booked to come in three times a day to see how we were doing and give Peter his morphine injections. We had seventeen more days.

During this time Mary and Phil sold their flat and, having delayed their departure to Canada for a month, moved into my mother's house. She was getting very frail and, as Mary by then was not working, they collected her from the nursing home and, together with the faithful housekeeper, they looked after her. Phil breezed in every evening and was a tonic. He was the only person with whom Peter was willing to be left with if I needed to go out at all. My sister-in-law, Diana, kept the family cared for.

Peter was slowly starving to death. He could not even swallow water and I was worried he would die in great pain with kidney failure. He did however manage to swallow a few sips of beer. I believe the alcohol cut through the cancer. So two or three times a day I sent one of the boys to the pub on the corner with a half-pint mug. By the thirteenth day he had had enough and, when the nurse came to give him his morphine, asked her to give him extra. She got very distressed and wrote in her report that he should be in hospital and told me that I was being very unfair to the children. It certainly was not harming Martin, who spent hours cuddled up with his Dad, watching T.V. or taking his puppy up to see him. "Go and have a cup of tea, Mummy—I'll look after Daddy," I was told frequently. The next day Peter's mood had completely changed. In the afternoon I had to go and see the bank manager and left Peter with his sister. When I got back she was desperately trying to find the vicar's phone number as Peter had demanded to see him without delay. When I asked what this was all about, the answer came: "I want to see if He'll have me back." I rang and the vicar came immediately, bless him. I left them together for what seemed an age. It was weeks since I had been out of Peter's sight for so long. Finally the vicar came to ask me to go and have Communion with Peter. I will never know what took place that afternoon; I only know that many years later the vicar told me it was the most amazing experience of his ministry. For his part, Peter seemed to have no more pain, wanted to be up in his chair all next day, laughed and joked with everyone who came near him and thoroughly enjoyed the show jumping on T.V. on Tuesday evening, frequently lifting his emaciated hand to give the famous Harvey Smith V sign. On Wednesday he gradually became weaker and after the nurse had given him his evening morphine went to sleep. I crept in beside him and spent the night listening to his every breath. The breathing got louder and louder and at 6 o'clock, I rang the nurse who came, gave him more morphine, and stayed with me while he died.

We laid him out, leaving his face uncovered and the nurse departed. Martin heard the commotion so I took him into the garden and told him Daddy had died but to please not wake the others. I heard a yell and wanted to scold him for waking his brother. "I don't like Daddy with his glasses off," he said. Peter was so short-sighted that he hated his glasses off and often slept a lot of the time with them on. I doubt whether Martin had ever seen them off before. "Go and put them on then," I said. He did and then sat on the bed by his dead father reading his comic. How well children cope with death. Later the vicar came and we had prayers round the bed. The funeral director was wonderful and spent a lot of time with all the children. I would like to have had Peter back until the funeral but wondered if the older children and Diana could cope. I was given permission to walk in and out of the funeral parlour, and to open and close the coffin as I liked whenever they were open. On the last day I cut a lock of his hair, put two buds from his favourite rose in his hand and closed the coffin for the last time.

We had a requiem with our wedding hymns and, as I returned from Communion, I laid my hand on the coffin and, from that moment our love, which had been both physical and spiritual, became spiritual and sacramental, and thus it has always been. I disposed that day of his clothes and gave away his personal possessions. He has no grave although he is in many Books of Remembrance. His memorial is his children and the grandchildren he never knew in this life. Anything I do for them is for us both. I could never confine his memory to a place but I talk to him often. A few weeks after the funeral I was stupid enough to run out of petrol at the bottom of a hill. As I trudged up the road with a can to the garage at the top I heard him laughing at my stupidity and I laughed too. Next day I was made a Tupperware manager and was given a smart new Avenger to drive!!

21

MUMMY DIES

After Peter's funeral, I had a lot of time to spend with Mummy, and with the family. Within three weeks, we were all at the airport waving off Mary and Phil to Canada. It was very hard for us all. Mary knew she would never see her grandmother again, and none of us knew how long it would be before we would next meet. I just did not know how I was going to cope without them, but desperately did not want anything to spoil their adventure. They rang me often in the nest few weeks. I had arranged for them to be met in Toronto by Ines and her husband, David, and they were to spend some time with them while they got settled. As it happened, they flew back before the end of the year to sort out various things, so it wasn't as bad as we had feared.

Mummy was in bed for most of the time by now. One morning, she announced that she had had a letter from my godmother's employers to say that she had died. She was my father's cousin, and, since his death, contact had been little more than a Christmas card. Irene had always been a nanny to a family in the north, caring for the children of three generations, and was looked after by the last family after her retirement. It appeared that I was now the only living relative and her few treasured possessions were to come to me. The funeral had already been arranged and there was little chance of my getting to that, but she wished to be buried with her parents in Kent. I went down to Tunbridge Wells to arrange to meet the coffin off the train and attend the burial. The undertakers were also able to bring me some silver and other items, which had been left to me. Whilst in Kent, I was also able to go to Farnborough to arrange for the burial of Peter's ashes in the garden of remembrance near his parents and first wife. I collected his ashes and took the family down to Farnborough at the weekend for a family day out.

By this time, we had all taken up residence in Mum's flat although I had to go home several times a day to get the boys to school and see to the dogs. Both lads were very unhappy in their schools; Julian because the school had just become comprehensive and trebled in size making it very impersonal. He was just approaching a second very close bereavement in a month and he had an enormous chip on his shoulder against all authority. I feared he would get completely out of control. Martin had been forced to change school, had few friends and was being bullied. On the plus side, Clare had given up her dubious relationship with a married man and had met a nice young fellow who was a sailor on nuclear submarines, but who was hoping to leave the Royal Navy within a year or two. He came from Carlisle, which was too far away for his shorter leaves, and so he spent quite a lot of time with us. He was with us on the night Mummy died and it was good to have a man around.

Unlike Peter who was conscious and talking to me until his last few minutes, Mum spent her final week mostly in a coma. She looked very peaceful and I think the children thought she was asleep. On the night she died, I sat by her bed from the time the evening nurse left until about 4 o'clock in the morning. I talked to her and watched her, and tried to keep awake. There was a comfortable chair on the other side of the room and I walked across there and sat with my eyes shut for a few minutes. When I returned to the bed, Mother was dead. I felt so guilty, but now know that what I did was right, because, in walking away, I was giving her permission to go. This experience was to become very important to me in my later ministry to the relatives of the dying. I have discovered that many people hang on to this life, although they long to go, just because they do not want to leave their loved ones grieving. Probably everyone, at some point, has to say goodbye and walk away and allow their loved one to go. I have been told since, by several people, that a parent or partner has asked, "Please, let me go." Dying is something we all have to do alone and we have to leave others the space to do it.

Mummy wanted to be buried with Sheila and my brother in Morden Cemetery, so I asked Diana, who lived in Morden, if we could use her house before and after the service, which was to take place in the cemetery chapel. Mum's vicar was unable to come, but he wrote a very good tribute to her, which the duty minister was able to use, but I found it all rather sad and uninspiring. Also, on going through some of her things, I had discovered that Sheila had had an illegitimate son, which Mother would have found out about when going through Sheila's things, something she never felt able to share with me, or even with my father. I know Sheila would have been far too scared ever to tell our parents, although I think she was pretty close to telling me on the night before my wedding. How lonely people were in their problems in those days. I told Mum's two younger sisters after the funeral and they were very understanding, but I was angry and upset. I have been trying to track down my nephew in New Jersey ever since, but doubt if I ever will. I imagine he was adopted. How I detest family secrets, or any other secrets for that matter: they are part of the darkness that we humans like to live in. If only we could bring things into the light: but I suppose that is impossible until we learn to forgive one another.

After my spate of funerals, I struggled on with my Tupperware parties and keeping my team together. I enjoyed having a good car and sold the Dormobile. Peter was well insured, the little house became mine, and I received £11,000, which in those days was a fortune. The children settled down, and I settled to a busy life with Tupperware, dogs, the various activities of our local church and planning for Christmas. I still had not cried, and was like a wound up spring. I think Clare and Julian realised that there was something wrong as they kept playing me Peter's favourite music. Then, one day, I had a really bad attack of my old friend, Paroxysmal Tachycardia. I lay down on the floor nearly all day, vomiting and in too much pain to move. Two days later would be Christmas Eve, and Roger, thinking it would be good for us all to have lots of people about, was coming with two of his friends. I struggled to start getting the house ready for them and collapsed again with another attack. Roger arrived, was embarrassed that his friends should see the state of the house, and he was very furious with me. Clare and Julian made themselves scarce and Martin hovered round me. To my visitors' credit, they set to, washed up, went shopping, and Roger cooked Christmas dinner and fed the family. I remember very little about the day except being in unbearable pain. I doubt I ever got to church that Christmas. I still had not cried.

The holiday over, I went to the doctor. He wanted to put me on Valium, but I refused, so he changed my heart tablets instead. I was convinced I just had to pull myself together, walked out of the doctor's and into Thomas Cook's, and booked to take the boys to Toronto on the first cheap flight of the year, on Freddie Laker's 'Skytrain'. We would go and see Mary in her new home, and hopefully see Ines in Ottawa as well. I had several more attacks of angina, but the new pills agreed with me and the attacks were milder and more manageable. Meanwhile, we were to change house.

22

THE GUINEA PIG SURVIVES AGAIN

There were no two ways about it—Knowsley Road was just too small for us. We were all under one another's feet and we would never be straight. I had got rid of some furniture, but the rooms were just not big enough. The vicar of Cosham, who had become such a good friend to us during the last traumatic six months, tried to get me to move from Knowsley Road into a house on the Highbury Estate, which constituted his parish. At the time we were living out of the parish although worshipping at St Philip's. It meant yet another change of school for Martin, but as he showed no sign of settling where he was I would risk it and hope he would be happier at Highbury. I think he found it worse! We found a lovely house with an extra big bedroom built in the roof space, which gave the boys a lot of room. Thinking back now, I believe it was the nicest house we have ever lived in, and I would go back there tomorrow given the chance. It was near a railway line and, far from finding the night trains disturbing, I found them quite comforting on my lonely sleepless nights. I spent some of the insurance money on getting the house as I wanted it and found it just right for the family and the dogs. Later, after we had had our holiday in Canada, I took in a student to help with the bills and we were all very happy apart from poor Martin's endless bullying at school. It is very hard for a parent to get the right balance in trying to help a child who is being bullied, particularly a boy. One wants them to be tough and stand up for themselves, but not to turn into bullies themselves. It is probably just as difficult for teachers.

Now settled in our new house, we left Clare and Paul in charge of the canine family, which was now fairly small, and, on the Friday before Good Friday, the boys and I flew to Toronto and stayed with Mary and Phil. They now had a very nice apartment and were getting things just as they wanted them. They had to work during the day but we managed to get out and about and the boys soon made friends with other youngsters in the road, and I enjoyed a rest. On Good Friday we all drove to Ines and Dave's for Easter together; and then Mary and Phil returned to work for the week leaving us to spend Easter week with Ines and coming back for us the following weekend when they had a week's holiday. It was a wonderful week in Ottawa and Ines and I chatted as though we had never been apart from each other for twenty years. On the last night, before leaving Ines, we all went out for a final meal together. On our return to the house, and, no doubt, aided by a few Irish coffees, I suddenly had an overwhelming feeling that here I was with my best friend from childhood and Peter had never known her, and now never would. At last the floodgates were open and I cried as I have never before or since wept in my life. It was the accumulation of eight months tension and I thought I would never stop. Everyone was wonderful and gave me space, realising how necessary it was for my sanity. Next morning, I felt much better, but was sorry Ines had such a watery ending to our holiday. Oh the blessed relief of tears!

Later that day we left Ottawa and drove home to Toronto the long way, crossing into the States, spending a night at Albany and then going to see the Great Lakes on the way home. Three days later we were heading back to England. Phil was wonderful with my two fatherless boys, taking them out to fly kites, taking them to McDonald's, which was the new phenomenon, and playing cricket. We also had a wonderful day in a nature park where we drove amongst sunbathing lions and had monkeys dance on the car, and put their hands through the window to pinch our sandwiches. It was wonderful. Later in the year I paid for Clare and her boyfriend Paul to go out to visit Mary and Phil. I then used the last of the money to enable Phil's parents to go. We could now all visualise them in their home and I don't think any of us felt they were very far away after that.

Back in England I knew we all had to settle down and I had to make plans for the future. Peter had said to me many times when he was dying that he wanted me to go back into Ministry. But how? Things had changed so much in the church and the chances of my now being accepted to train as a deaconess were very remote. I went to see the chairman of the Board of Women's work and was told I could not work full time while I had two children still at school and I would have to go to another selection centre if I still wished to be a deaconess. A few days later she rang me to ask if I was interested in a part-time post in a parish, which was close enough to where I lived for me not to have to move. I went to see the vicar, who informed me he was a great champion of women's work, and he would be keen to help with the boys as he had a serving team of lads in whom he took a great interest. I would only have to work two or three days a week although he would like me at the daily Eucharist as far as possible. For this I would be paid £1000 a year, which even by the standards of the seventies was very little. However, apart from the money, it seemed a way back into ministry and I felt I could manage. Before I could take up the post I was back in hospital. Peter Thomas, our vicar in Cosham, came to visit me and to see what he could do. Someone must have appeared to look after Martin but I was desperately worried about Julian and begged Peter to keep an eye on him as he was running wild. For the sake of the children I persuaded the doctor to send me home, promising to bed rest at home. I was brought home by ambulance and had been in the house an hour, when Martin opened the door to a policewoman who had come to inform me that Julian had been charged with two friends for trashing a local school and was at the police station. There was nothing for it but to get dressed, leave Martin in the care of a neighbour and go with the policewoman. I brought my erring son home to await junior court proceedings.

After several days bed rest and another change in my heart tablets I was a lot better and, by the time the date had arrived for me to start at Stamshaw, I was really quite well. My new employer seemed very kind and gave us a lovely requiem for Peter on the anniversary of his death. He also came to court with me, and spoke on Julian's behalf. It was quite horrific what the boys had done to the school and Julian was given two years community service. I am sure it was not his idea but, once the decision had been made to break in, he admitted to taking over the leadership role, and was given rather more punishment than the other two lads. He is still a leader, and now puts this quality to good use. He took his punishment manfully, although I think most of it was spent marching about rather than doing anything constructive with all his hours of community service. Later, when Julian himself had a job looking after lads on community service, they were doing the useful things they are known for today.

During all this time I was facing another crisis over my mother's estate. When she died she was living in the basement of a huge block of flatlets, mostly lived in by elderly people. She had bought it some years before as a going concern and had run it most successfully with the help of Miss Sainsbury, the faithful soul whom I have referred to previously, and who kept an eye on the place in return for free accommodation. During Mother's illness several of the flats became empty and were not advertised and I was just too tied up to do anything about it. Mum had quite a lot of good furniture and possessions and as it was impossible for me to spend much time there, I was looking for a caretaker for the place. In the end I heard of a young couple, the daughter and son in law of a friend of a friend. They seemed a pleasant enough young couple and I agreed to let them live there rent-free if they took over the running of the place. An added bonus was that the young man was quite a handyman and would look after any jobs that might need doing around the place.

At first things could not have gone better. They were a pleasant couple and we were able to let some of the empty flats. My suspicions were first aroused in two ways. Miss Sainsbury took a great dislike to them, which I thought at first was jealousy and, every time I visited them in their flat, I noticed little things were missing. We had done an inventory before they came in, so I was not too worried and, if I remarked on anything, was told that the item had been put away for safety. Meanwhile my solicitor was trying to sell the property for me through business agencies. Few people seemed interested. Meanwhile the building was deteriorating fast, and the occupants of the flat seemed to be more and more difficult. I then discovered that, unbeknown to me, they had allowed some other young people into the one or two empty flats and shouting and loud music was causing trouble with some of the older occupants. Finally, the gable end was blown off the block in a Southsea gale. I was therefore very relieved when my solicitor rang me to say he had had an offer of £18,000 for the place just as it was. It was to be turned into an old peoples' retirement home and the purchasers would do all that was necessary to get it up and running. They would also allow the one or two long-term elderly folk who had flats there, including Miss Sainsbury, to stay for the rest of their lives. It seemed too good to be true although I knew I would lose a lot of money. I could also, if I wished, have their house, which was just round the corner from the church where I was now working, in part-exchange. It was a dilemma. Should I stay in the house that I liked so much and share my allegiance between the two churches, or move yet again into this huge Victorian house on Northern Parade and throw myself completely into this new parish. News that the Thomases had itchy feet and were hoping to move to Kent, and the fact that this huge house gave me further scope to supplement my meagre earnings with lodgers and dog breeding, decided it for me, and reluctantly we moved.

Within a few weeks I was very ill again and returned to Guy's Hospital where they suggested I have further heart surgery. Advances in heart surgery during the thirty years since those early pioneering days of my first operation were enormous, and the risks nominal by comparison. I was to have a 'Total Correction', during which time my heart would be stopped and I would be put on a bypass. They would then be able to correct and complete the first operation, which had served me so well. However, I was still being a guinea pig as this attempt to complete the early operations had not been done before. I do not know if any others of those first few would have been alive by then anyway. I had to go in a number of times for short periods, for tests and, finally, for the operation. There were no more oxygen tents, no more paralysis and no more aspirations, but I was told that when I came round I would be on a ventilator and would have probes and tubes in every orifice in my body. However, I would recover quickly and be home within a fortnight. All was true, but I will never forget the fear I sustained when I woke in the ICU and could not breathe for myself. I longed for my faithful friend the oxygen tent. Great care was taken in the hospital to let the next of kin of patients see the rooms in intensive care, and all the equipment involved. Because Clare had just started as a junior nurse in the hospital, no one thought to take her round or even warn her in advance and, when she saw me, she nearly had a fit. The hospital admitted they had clanged and the Sister Tutor was very understanding. Arrangements had to be made for the care of the boys and the dogs while I was in hospital, and some friends offered. They had two youngsters, the elder a friend of Martin. They coped for three weeks, which enabled me to have a week's convalescence with the Thomases in their new parish in Bromley. It was good to have them so near to the hospital, and to be able to spend a week with them on my way home. Clare and a friend of hers came to collect me to go home. As soon as I walked into the house the others walked out. They had had enough. Clare had to return to work, Julian had started his first job and I was still very weak. Hazel, Clare's friend, managed to arrange to have a few days to help me get on my feet. She was wonderful and I just do not know how I could have survived those first few days without her. I improved rapidly. It was the total correction I needed and the fact that I am writing this at seventy-five shows how successful it was.

I returned to work, took over the local branch of the Mothers' Union (I had been involved at diocesan level for many years and was chairman of the overseas department), started a very thriving cub pack from which the vicar drew his young servers, and started a lunch club for the elderly with help from our own M.U. and the League of Catholic Mothers. I soon discovered that one just cannot work for God part-time, whatever the Church likes to say. I also found that the vicar had just no intention of allowing me to do anything in church although the male Reader was treated as a deacon. I had far more encouragement from our local R.C. priest, an Anglican convert who was chairman of the council of churches. I became his secretary and at the next election was voted chairman. At that time Derek Warlock was the R.C. Bishop of Portsmouth and a great believer in ecumenism. We were devastated when God sent him to Liverpool to work with David Shepherd, to save Liverpool from the terrible situation we are so familiar with in Northern Ireland. Those two famous bishops really did work a miracle and must never be forgotten.

Also, during our time at Northern Parade, Clare was married. I was determined that even without her dad I would do all I could to make sure she had a wedding as good as Mary's had been. My vicar was helpful, refusing to take any of the normal church fees. I made all the dresses for her and all her retinue of bridesmaids. Paul had a large family and all his three girl cousins wanted to be included. In the end she had six bridesmaids, a matron of honour and Paul's little seven-year-old brother as pageboy. It necessitated several journeys from Portsmouth to Liverpool for measuring and fitting, but the effort was well worth it. My cousin, Clare's godfather, came over from the Isle of Wight to give her away and the day went very well. Twenty-six of Paul's family arrived in a minibus. I managed to find outside accommodation for those who wanted it but the majority slept on floors, sofas, etc, and the children slept on mattresses under the billiard table in Martin's basement bedroom. Clare and Paul borrowed my car and went off for a touring holiday. Strangely enough, they spent a lot of time in Great Yarmouth, which they loved. Little did they know what a large part in all our lives Yarmouth was to play.

I worked hard, enjoyed all I did but financially I was desperate. I looked after students for a pittance and struggled with my Cavalier and Peke bitches. I exported the first Ruby Cavalier to go to the States and bred a lovely stud dog offering to whelp his puppies for a pittance. After four years I had to sell my only asset, my house, to survive.

23

GREAT YARMOUTH, HERE WE COME

Alongside my struggle to keep a roof over our heads, I was looking for full-time work. I drove all over the country to interviews in a variety of dioceses. Twice I was offered what seemed an ideal post with clergy house as a bonus, only to have it turned down later. I must explain: in those days, in order to be accepted for a post, one first of all had to be offered it by the local incumbent; then it had to be approved by the diocesan bishop and finally by the Board of Women's Work of that particular diocese—and therein was the rub. It was at this stage I was turned down. I do not think my sisters in the Church had fully forgiven me for leaving the fold to get married. I know there was some jealousy and a feeling that I was seeking to get the best of both worlds and, in getting married, had not been willing to accept the necessary singleness of mind and purpose those called to ministry should be willing to offer. I, on the other hand, felt that the experience of eighteen years of the give and take of marriage, and of being both a mother and a stepmother, had made me a far more rounded and far less precious person than I had been when first in ministry.

I was nervous that my present employer should discover that I was disappearing from time to time and would twig that I was job hunting. In the end my fears were realised and, after a somewhat tense meeting, he agreed to give me three months notice. We now had to move fast!

As the end of term arrived I decided to concentrate on selling the big house and getting a full-time job again, hopefully with a clergy house of some sort. Julian, after a rather turbulent patch, had gone back to college and was courting seriously. Whatever I did, I would concentrate on Martin and me. He left his junior school in July 1979 and I had to decide where he was to go in the September. I had heard of a little private school of only about 80 boys which a friend had sent her son to and where there was a lot of individual attention. The headmaster

GREAT YARMOUTH, HERE WE COME

was one of the old school and I felt that Martin had been bullied so much and was so vulnerable that, although I would have to pay, this would be the best solution for him until I knew where we were going. He was extremely happy there and in the six months he was there he regained a lot of the confidence he had been lacking.

I eventually sold the house and found a derelict little house with no proper kitchen or bathroom and where an old lady had lived and died and nothing had been done to it for ages. At the time I bought it we still had a labour government and handsome grants were being given for houses that needed a bathroom. I put in for a grant and was awarded one of £4000, which was very good in those days. I had plans drawn up by an architect and approved by the council for what promised to be a very nice little house. As my future movements were so unknown and I had to make provision for both boys in the event of my death, I had the deeds and a small mortgage in both Julian's name and mine. I would pay their mortgage while he was at college and then hopefully if he got married he could buy me out and start married life in a nice house. Coming home from church a few days later I found all the steps leading to our front door covered in boxes, bags and pot plants. Sandy, Julian's girlfriend, had been chucked out of her home. There was no alternative but to take her in and I tried to contact her mother. She came to see me late that night and said she would take her back only if she promised never to see Julian. I never could make out the reason for such hostility but I think some of it was because he had helped her contact her real father. On the day we moved out of Northern Parade and into 6 Target Road, most of my belongings had to go into store and with an absolute minimum of possessions the boys, Sandy and I lay down on cushions and sleeping bags in the only habitable bedroom and wondered what we had done. There was gas in the house and the next day I bought two gas fires and an electric ring for cooking. A few weeks later Julian and Sandy had had enough and found themselves a flat and Clare and Paul had moved in!

In October I went to yet another interview, this time in Great Yarmouth which held such happy memories for Clare and Paul. There was just too much going on to be away overnight and I still had animals needing care and attention. It was too far to drive in one day and I had had so many set-backs that I was not very hopeful, so decided to leave on the first train of the day which would get me to Yarmouth just after lunchtime and would give me just four hours there. The vicar met me and it was the strangest interview I have ever had in my life. I was asked not one question about myself, but taken on a whistle stop tour of the five churches and told their history and the history of the town. I was then taken to see over the six-bedroomed parsonage, which would be my home, and to have a cup of tea with the young curate who had just finished serving his title and was moving to a second curacy. He and his wife were charming and the vicar left us alone for a little while to chat. Then on to Evening Office in the huge parish church of St Nicholas, where I met the parish clerk and a warden; and then to the Vicarage to meet the vicar's wife, a doctor, and to have a good meal. The conversation was small talk and then I was whisked to the station to catch my train.

Vicar: "I would like you to come and start as soon as possible."

Me: "What about the Board?"

Vicar: "She's a friend of mine, leave her to me."

Me: "What about the Bishop?"

Vicar: "I have already spoken to him, and he remembers you when you were in Hackney and he was married to Marjorie; but, as he knows you, he thinks it would be good for you to see the Archdeacon."

Me: "I shall have to think about it and talk it over with the family."

At that moment my train arrived. When I got home and made enquiries I found that Richard had been in touch with almost everyone he could think of in Portsmouth and knew almost more about me than I know myself! The family were very supportive and Martin took the test for Yarmouth Grammar School and passed it. Clare and Paul found themselves a little house in Fratton and, when we went, Julian and Sandy gave up their flat and moved back in. Julian drove the three of us, four dogs and an enormous cheese plant, my pride and joy, all the way to Yarmouth. As we drove away, the council were shovelling building materials into the front room that I had used as a study!

The good thing about going into such a large parsonage was that I was able to get all my furniture and all that I still had of Mum's out of store and get it sorted out. Our welcome in Yarmouth was excellent and, after being welcomed at the vicarage with a huge meal, we went to the house to find a fire blazing in the grate. We saw to the dogs and spread sleeping bags on the floor and went to bed. Next morning we moved in.

I was hoping to have a couple of weeks to settle in before starting work but it was only a day or two before the vicar came to ask me if I could do a funeral in three days time, as neither he nor the curate were available. Panic! I had never taken a funeral in my life, and this was not an informal crematorium affair, but was to be in St Nicholas's Church with burial afterwards. My main concern was what I should wear and what part the Parish Clerk was to play in the service. In actual fact I need not have worried about him as he and the undertakers were so used to working together that all I needed was to slot myself in as we moved around the Church. I had been warned that they probably all felt that a woman would be a threat to their beautiful pageantry and I had to give the impression that I had been doing it all my life.

The problem of what to wear was a more serious one. Parish workers at that time mostly wore maroon cassocks or maroon gowns like choirgirls often wear, and I definitely preferred a cassock. I had ordered one as soon as I knew we were going to Great Yarmouth, but it had not arrived. When it did, it was the wrong size and very badly made. A quick phone call to the board secretary and I managed to borrow one. Luckily, I was able to keep this one until able to change it for my deaconess cassock two years later. In the end, the funeral went quite well, and my ministry to Great Yarmouth had begun. Over the next seven years I was to do an average of four funerals a week.

It did not take me long to realise that, once again, God was using me as a Guinea Pig. The vicar was a great champion of women's work, and had been to China and met the first Anglican lady to be ordained priest. He had been so impressed by her that he was determined to have women priests in the Anglican Church throughout the world. For my part, it was good to be treated as an experienced member of staff, to have my Church family at St. John's to care for, and to take full share in preaching and singing the offices in St. Nicholas's Church with their wonderful choir. It is true that I did find my niche, and many, in all the churches, who had at first regarded me with superstition, quickly got used to having this funny looking woman about the place. One or two left, but many others came to take their place, some, no doubt, out of curiosity. It was a time of great change. The Cathedral wanted to start having women servers and vergers and girls in the choir, and I believe such experiments were tried out first in the big churches like St. Nicholas and its sister church of St. Peter Mancroft before being tried in the cathedral itself. It is hardly surprising that for many people there was a feeling of "When is it all going to end?"

24

LIFE GIRLS

It was strange for Martin and me to find ourselves living in this enormous house and I felt that such a wonderfully big house should be put to some use. By the time everything was out of store and I had sorted all my furniture, and Mum's, there was a number of possibilities open. I needed some help with the physical running of such a large house and started by taking in a homeless mum with her baby to live rent free in return for cooking and cleaning. She was a lovely Christian girl with a number of problems and I discussed with her the possibility of running a hostel for unmarried mothers. I had for many years been a member of "Life, save the unborn child" and had recently joined the Lowestoft branch. Within a month I was asked to take a seventeen-year-old pregnant mum who also came from Portsmouth. She was quickly followed by a number of others. "Life" worked out with me what they should pay towards their keep and they all chipped in and helped one another. In some cases, where they had no parent or boyfriend to be with them, I took them to hospital and stayed with them throughout the birth. We all got on extremely well and were one big happy family. It was a wonderful arrangement. On one or two evenings a week, when I was free, I would baby-sit for the girls so that they could go out, and they confided in me a great deal, which was very rewarding. Their families and boyfriends were always made welcome and I enjoyed helping them with the babies, while Martin seemed to enjoy having such a large number of big sisters. Inevitably there were lots of opportunities to talk about faith and the Church and one or two asked me to baptise their babies. I tried hard to get them to come to services at St John's, but they seemed afraid of even the most informal worship. However two of them went to the Greek Orthodox Church from time to time, I think because all their services seem to have no beginning or end and there is freedom to wander in and out at will.

Three months after our arrival at Yarmouth, "Life" sent me a much older woman who was pregnant. We were by then quite full up and all I had was a little room on the second floor over the landing. She did not fit in in any way with the others and seemed to spend most of her time in a local pub. One day I conducted a funeral at St John's and on my return from the crematorium could not get into the house, front or back. Fortunately the young organist was around and climbed in through a window to let me in. We were having a social for the Young Wives group in the evening and while I was preparing for this, Catherine came in and told me that she had been chased by a young man while returning from a midday drink at the pub, and had run home and locked all the doors. She seemed quite distressed and I suggested she stayed in for the rest of the day.

The social over, we all went to bed. At about four o'clock I woke to find a young man of Middle Eastern appearance holding a wooden mallet over my head. I started to scream, but he put his hand over my mouth and my initial fear quickly gave way to reason. There had recently been a case of a family being held hostage by an Iranian with a grudge, and I feared we were going to be taken hostage. The only people in the house were Martin and two girls, one with a baby, and one very advanced in pregnancy, and all on the top floor. Those in the room next to mine were away for the weekend. I certainly did not want anyone frightened. I had to talk my way out of this. It turned out that he was not a hostage taker, but he was a rapist and was the young man from whom Catherine had fled the previous day. I managed to get the mallet away from him but refused to tell him which was Catherine's room. I then talked him through the night, allowed him to rape me, made him a cup of tea and got him out of the house without him going up to the others on the top floor. He struck me as a very inadequate young man with an enormous number of problems and desperately in need of help, but I had to ring the police for everyone's sake. What the police put me through was infinitely worse than anything that had happened during the night and I can well understand why so much rape goes unreported. I was cross-examined several times and made to feel I was a villain rather than someone trying to be a responsible citizen. I do not believe the police believed half of what I said and the medical examination was humiliating and degrading. The worst part of all was that I was not allowed time to say goodbye to Martin, who woke to find a policewoman standing by me, and then saw me driven away in a police car. What went through the poor boy's head I shudder to think. I believe, and hope, that things are a lot more sensitively dealt with today. All I can say is that what I went through was appalling. After five and a half hours of questioning I was told that I could go, although nobody was concerned how I got home. I had heard from a policewoman that it was in the lunchtime edition of the paper, my name had not been mentioned although my connection with the church had been seized upon. I asked if I could phone my vicar, as I wanted to tell him before he read it in the paper. I was also secretly hoping that although it was his day off, if he was around, he would come and take me home. My request was denied and I was shoved back in an interview room while the police sergeant rang on my behalf. The whole experience was now beginning to get the better of me and when, what seemed hours later, the vicar's doctor wife walked in, I broke down. The vicar was kindly but firmly sorting out the long arm of the law! The young man was shopped by an inmate of Norwich prison and caught the next day. He admitted the offence and I did not have to go to court. The bishop, the archdeacon and my spiritual director were wonderful and I soon healed from the experience; however, without them it might well have been a different story. I often wonder what happened to the young man. Around that time the news was about the Pope being taken to see his would-be assassin and I determined to try to visit the young man in jail. All I could find out was that he had been moved for his own safety and that his whereabouts were not to be revealed. If he ever reads this, which is doubtful, I want him to know I forgive him and hope he forgives me for doing what I had to do.

In the September of that year Martin and I returned to Portsmouth for the wedding of Julian and Sandy. They had had a very hard time after we left for Yarmouth. First of all, there had been a change of Government, and the promised £4000 to improve the house was reduced to £1200 and all the plans had to be pruned. Sandy's father was fantastic and worked with Julian to make the house really nice before the wedding and they moved in. Sadly, the marriage lasted only a matter of months, but the house is still in the family as Clare and her family have lived in it, improving it bit by bit, for over twenty years. They still seem very happy there. One of the guinea pig's more successful moves. My grandchildren, now in their twenties, have never known any other home, and I realise how they have benefited from this stability, as opposed to what I put my poor children through with my constant moving.

At the time that I joined the team at Yarmouth there was just the vicar, curate, two readers and me to serve five churches. As this was a teaching parish, the next to join us was a young deacon fresh from St Stephen's House. Like me, he was told that he had to do a funeral on the day after his arrival in the parish and had spent the whole of his ordination retreat worrying about it—hardly the best start to his ministry. In less than a week it became very obvious to me that he just was not coping and was extremely lonely. Weeks later he told me that he had made a big mistake and had spent his day off on the Isle of Wight wondering how to get out of it. Instead, he came to lunch the following Sunday, played snooker with the boys with whom he struck up a real friendship, and talked! I don't think that first year was particularly easy for him, but by the time he was priested he had gained a lot of confidence and was very popular in the parish. He even became very good at taking funerals! He served his second curacy in Birmingham where I visited him several times and we went together on a pilgrimage to the Holy Land, which was great fun, although we have drifted apart in the last ten years. I have often wondered how many young men and women who are alone in a new parish suffer as he did, and why there is not a better support system for them. I have been told that Deacons and Readers are now told of the importance of having a Spiritual Director, or a Soul Friend, in place, before leaving Theological College. I do hope this is always the case.

Eighteen months after we came to Yarmouth I was made a deaconess in St Nicholas Church. It was an unforgettable experience. I went away to Retreat for three days and then came back to have lunch with my old friend Bishop Maurice and his wife. We talked of the old days in Islington and caught up with each other's families. Most of my family arrived the next day and were accommodated in our big house, and on the evening of Candlemas I was made deaconess. All the local clergy came, even the Greek Orthodox priest who embarrassed poor Maurice by throwing himself at his feet and kissing his ring. The Youth Club made me a lovely blue cope to wear for all the processions we frequently had at St Nicholas' and I felt very loved and appreciated.

Being a deaconess made very little difference at first to what I did and for several months I continued to have the pastoral care of St John's and filled the house with "Life" girls. Unfortunately, the Church discovered that a great deal of money was needed to be spent on the parsonage at St John's and it was sold to the owners of the nursing home next door. I was asked to look for something smaller that the diocese could afford to buy for me. Believing that I should cost the church the minimum, I found a tiny little house, which was just large enough for Martin, my one remaining "Life" girl, the dogs and me. It had no garden and the dogs needed to be taken on the beach three times a day, but we were happy there for another eighteen months.

There was no room in this little house for Julian who was recovering from his broken marriage, but with the little bit of profit made when I sold the house in Portsmouth to Clare and Paul, I was able to buy a little cottage in Winterton. Again it needed a great deal done to it but, once the constructional work was done, we were able to decorate it ourselves and it gave me somewhere to get away on my day off as well as providing a comfortable home for Julian and a friend.

Winterton was a favourite village of mine and my first thoughts were to retire there, though it was not to be.

My concern for the plight of single mums stayed with me and for a while we tried to set up a home for the girls where they would support themselves. Many of them went into bed and breakfast accommodation during the winter months but were turned out during the day to wander the streets with their babies. A greater need seemed to be to supply somewhere that was warm and where they could make drinks, feed and change their babies and enjoy some company during the daytime. Through "Life", Gingerbread, the Girls' Life Brigade and Social Services, a project for single parents, was finally set up which has helped many, providing child care and even enabling some to get qualifications in a variety of fields. There is no longer the stigma attached to singe parents there was only fifteen years ago. I kept in touch with many of the girls for a number of years and still see one girl and her two teenage daughters very frequently.

25

THE GUINEA PIG IS BLESSED BY THE HOLY SPIRIT

Shortly before we came to Yarmouth, four young people, two Anglican and two Roman Catholic, who had been working in a hospice in London, felt that God was leading them to live in Community. The initial idea was that the two men would get jobs to support the venture, and the girls would run the house for whomever Social Services wanted to send to them for short or longer periods. A lot of prayer went into the venture and I would pop in from time to time to visit and to pray with them. Most of the people sent to them had deep psychological problems, or were social misfits. They lived in Community and had a very good structured but free life. The conversion of an outside sunroom to a tastefully arranged chapel was a great blessing and its regular use gave a focus to the day. Everyone who could was encouraged to play his or her part in the running of this very successful home. It all went very well until two of the original team left and other, well meaning but far less disciplined folk joined, and the standards started to slip. It still did a very good job, and many people were helped during their stay there, but things were not the same and, when I went in one day to find the chapel was now a tool shed, I was devastated.

Through my friendship with two of the original four I was led to a prayer group at the R. C. convent every Tuesday night. It was a charismatic group, but, unlike any experience I had previously had of charismatics, or renewal in any form, it was open to all and very friendly. Through this group I learned a lot about the Holy Spirit, and about being truly open to His Power and Healing Love, and my prayer life was drastically changed from top to bottom. I learned a lot about praising God for all things, good and bad, and about meditation and resting in the Spirit. In other words, I learned to trust God more than I ever had before. My ministry, too, had a new focus, and there were many times when I felt I could say with St. Paul, "It is no longer I who live but Christ who liveth in me."

There were many changes happening in the Church at this time, not least in the position of women in the Church of England. Many churches, even the most Anglo-Catholic, now welcomed women as Readers, and as servers, and women were frequently asked to preach. Both MOW (the Movement for the Ordination of Women) and WOW (Women against the Ordination of Women) were very active. I joined the latter briefly but found them very unconvincing. They seemed more concerned with the wearing of trousers or cutting one's hair than with the nature of priesthood. I was, however, an enthusiastic member of the Church Union which locally had a very good renewal ministry.

I took my experience of renewal very seriously and started a charismatic prayer group in the parish. I was also very involved in "Churches Together" and in anything that involved the churches of Yarmouth working together. On Good Friday every year we produced a tableau of Holy Week and Good Friday based, in a very humble way, on Oberammergau. All the churches were involved. I was therefore very concerned that nothing the Church of England did should rock the "Unity" boat.

I could see absolutely no reason why women should not become deacons; in fact, as a deaconess, I felt like a deacon as far as the Church was concerned and, at my vicar's request, I wore a deacon's stole, read the Gospel, and prepared the altar at communion, as well as training the young servers.

There had been yet another change around, and a new priest had joined the staff and would look after St John's and the other church in the south of the parish. I had therefore become far more based at the Parish Church which necessitated yet another move, this time into the considerably larger house in the centre of town. We had space to take in one or two more girls and we had a reasonable sized garden. Martin had by now left school and lived for snooker. He had adolescent dreams of becoming a professional and worked very hard at a variety of jobs to pay for his training. I did all I could to encourage him and to soften the blow when he slowly came to terms with the fact that he was not the natural he aspired to be. Fortunately he met the girl who later became his wife, and he discovered there were even better things in life than becoming a professional snooker player. I believe he suffered more than he ever let on to me, but he and Shelly had the strong relationship that enabled them to boost each other's confidence.

I also took on the role of Hospital Chaplain. This involved taking communion from the Reserved Sacrament to the sick, and ministering to the dying. I also tried to have an open door for the staff and befriended as many as possible, frequently eating with them in the refectory. I was very aware of the fact that I was not a priest and frequently found people confided in me things that required absolution and then having to ask the very understanding vicar to go and absolve them. As he was very deaf, it was difficult for him to listen to sick or quietly spoken people, so we operated as a team—me hearing confessions, and him giving absolution. For the first time I could not help feeling it might be helpful to the sick and dying to be able to anoint and give absolution but was still quite sure it was impossible. I would argue my corner with anyone.

As a somewhat political animal I found the role of deaconess very unsatisfactory; because we were not regarded as truly laity, we could not vote with the house of Laity in Synod and, as we were not truly ordained, we were not allowed to vote with the Clergy. Many people do not realise that to be a deaconess disenfranchises them and this certainly did not suit me. As a committed Anglo-Catholic, it seemed to me that it was more correct to have a woman in the deacon's position at Communion, where the Blessed Virgin stood at the offering of the Holy Sacrifice, as can be seen in any Rood Screen. Meanwhile, Portsmouth Diocese was experimenting with making men permanent deacons in line with the custom of the Roman Catholic Church. These were men who for some reason were not accepted by ACCM (the selection board of the day) for the priesthood, but were felt to have a very real ministry. The next obvious step was to recognise the deaconesses as clergy. There was little doubt that the vote to ordain women deacons would go fairly smoothly through all houses in Synod. However, due to the fact that the country was at war in the Falklands, it was years before the matter could seem to be of enough importance to be discussed in Parliament. We waited and waited and waited, frequently feeling frustrated and disappointed. It seemed, to many of us, surprising that a woman Prime Minister should be so little bothered about her sisters in the established church.

In my naive way I believed that once all the deaconesses were ordained we would truly have a proper third order in the church, and I joined a group which was praying for a permanent diocanate (male and female) and was active in the Roman Catholic Church, the Lutheran Church and others. I desperately hoped that the Anglican Church would take a lead in this. I hoped that deaconesses, readers, senior religious and others, many of whom were as well, if not better trained than many priests were, would all be brought together and ordained into the third order. Silly me. I should have known that this was far too simple for the Church of England which is never content unless making things as complicated as possible. Nor had I bargained for the strength of MOW.

It became more and more obvious to me that if I was accepted for ordination, then I would probably be approaching 60 by then and, in those days women retired and drew their pension at sixty. I knew the vicar, proud as he was of having a teaching parish and not at the time having a deacon, dreamed of having a woman straight from theological college. I also believe he wanted one who was committed to fighting to become a priest. I therefore started to look at parishes. Martin was soon to marry and, as he and I had been so dependent on one another since Peter's death, I felt it would be good for his marriage to put some distance between us. I went and stayed with Kevin, the young curate I had been to Israel with, and looked at a parish near his in Birmingham. I was offered the post and spent a weekend in the parish, then went home, gave in my notice, and started to pack up. I knew by then that I would be ordained in June 1987, three days after my sixtieth birthday. A few weeks later I had a letter to say that due to unexpected parish reorganisation they would have to have a second priest and I was no longer required.

I was now in a real dilemma. Yarmouth had been told I was going and another woman had been interviewed to take my place and live in my house. I went to see the bishop. Poor Bishop Peter had only been in the Diocese for about eighteen months and it seemed that most of his time had been spent sorting out the deaconesses and others who were to be ordained. There were going to be far more deacons than he could possibly hope to find parishes for. He begged the vicar to let me stay on at Yarmouth as a non-stipendiary, but I realised this would be very difficult for the new deacon and me. I told the Bishop I would try and get a post outside Norwich Diocese.

The next week the following advert appeared in the *Church Times*—"59 year old experienced deaconess, due to be ordained at Petertide, is looking for a parish where she can be used. Catholic background, Charismatic, Willing to go anywhere in the country." I had two replies. One was from an Anglo Catholic Priest who had a daughter church in his parish which was in partnership with the Methodists. They had had a Methodist minister who had just left and he was anxious to replace him with an Anglican deacon. He then informed me that about twenty had already replied and they were not interviewing until May. The other was from a parish in the Salcombe Estuary, which seemed a very long way away.

I took a couple of days and went to Devon. The benefice was a beautiful area between Kingsbridge and Salcombe. The parish church and vicarage were in Malborough. There was an assistant priest in West Alvington, the town end of the parish, and there had been up to this point a vacancy for a retired priest to serve the coastal area of Galmpton and Hope Cove on a "House for duty" basis. The previous two retired Priests had only stayed a few months, largely, I think, because of the unsuitable housing. In all, nine men had been to look at the villages and the two churches, but none seemed to want to come or were thought suitable. The area is quite wealthy, and in the past the people of the villages had bought their own parsonage. However, as the congregation became smaller, and the house was becoming an added responsibility, they had sold it and bought a bungalow, which had been built as a holiday home. To make it more suitable, the main room had been enlarged and a porch built, but it was hardly the dream retirement home for a retiring clergy couple to live out their last days of ministry by the sea.

To my surprise I knew almost at once that I would come—when one of the wardens told me that one Sunday afternoon, feeling quite desperate about her corner of the benefice, she had gone into the little Chapel of Ease at Hope Cove to pray about it. After a while she had heard what she always believed was the voice of God saying to her, "What this place needs is a woman." Shortly after she got home the vicar rang her to come with the other warden to look at an advert he had read in the *Church Times*! I think we could all see the hand of God at work and it fitted well with my guinea pig status.

After a very enjoyable two days, in which I met many encouraging and friendly people including the Bishop of Plymouth, I went back to Yarmouth to continue packing up. Then, one evening, Derek, the Vicar of Malborough, rang me to say that the Rural Dean and several of the other clergy were giving him a hard time because he was appointing a woman deacon. He was still happy for me to come and so were most people in the benefice, but the deanery were going to prove a different story. I said that I was happy if he was happy, but also that I was glad I had been warned.

I went into my ordination retreat on my sixtieth birthday. After two days we came out of silence on the Saturday afternoon to try on our clerical shirts and dog collars, two men and about twenty assorted women, from ancient point of retirement deaconesses like me to young mums who were worried how their children were going to behave in the cathedral. It turned out to be quite a mannequin parade and there was much merriment until supper when we all went solemnly back into silence. Next morning, after breakfast, we were driven to the cathedral for the Ordination of Deacons service. The Bishop was very anxious that the men and women be ordained deacon together and made the priests wait another week. I think Norwich was the only diocese to handle things this way, but it seemed to me to augur well for the future of the diaconate.

Ordination and photographs over, I could greet my family. I had gone to considerable trouble to organise lunch for us all at a small restaurant in Norwich which was willing to do Sunday lunch. I think the proprietor's ambitions were more than she could cope with, or else some of her staff had let her down. The service was exceedingly slow and halfway through we were told that the cook had collapsed and Clare went to give first aid. The cook was carted away in an ambulance and we all had to adjourn down the road to the Pizza bar for the rest of our meal. In the evening I was to preach at my swan song at St Nicholas, Great Yarmouth. I said in my sermon that three great things had happened to me during my time in Yarmouth: I had become a deaconess in that very church, I had been that morning ordained deacon, and I had become a grandmother. The service ended with Juliet and Christopher, my two grandchildren, joining me in the pulpit and everyone sang "How great thou art." It was an amazing day. One week later I was on my way to Devon.

26

DOGS

During my last few years in Great Yarmouth I had done quite well with the Bernese Mountain dogs we kept. It was a love that Martin and I could share and enjoy together. Zoe, our original bitch who really belonged to Julian, lived with us until she was quite elderly and was finally put to sleep lying in the garden with her head on my lap. Her daughter Heidi was Martin's dog and she gave us two large litters of pups, which we sold well. In her first litter, which were mostly boys, one rather mismarked little girl went to a friend of Clare's and the other to a local family who already had a very promising dog pup and with whom we later became friendly and went to many shows together. We kept the big boy, who was the last one born. He appeared a very promising dog and I took to showing him quite regularly. In the end he qualified for Cruft's where he got two seconds. I came home walking on air. A dog that my friend had bred got the reserve ticket. I promptly booked to have a bitch of the same breeding should one ever become available. My dream was to mate her with my Teddy and start my own line.

My last Cavalier had died and, apart from Teddy, we just had two rescued bitches. First my little mismarked girl turned up in Bernese rescue. The marriage had broken up and poor little Bess had been passed on two or three times. By the time I bought her back she was nervous and had a suspect temperament. Martin and Shelly had her many years, and, with love and a strong hand, she became a delightful well-behaved dog, and outlived the rest of the litter. My daughter's stupid friend went and got another Bernese and again could not cope. I bought the Bitch from her and had some pups from her to prove Teddy, but their hips were faulty and I had her spayed. In the end Clare had her and again she lived to a good old age. Meanwhile, the bitch puppy I had wanted from my friend's dogs had arrived. I called her Bella after my very first Cavalier, and she, I believed, was to be the start of a new era. I was taking to Devon a pair of wonderful Bernese that were to experience the good life, and my beautiful tabby cat. All I needed to make my family complete was a Border Collie to live indoors with me. I found my pup, a beautiful brown and white smooth collie, and we were ready for the new life. It was not going to be that simple, however. I had heard bad news of some of Teddy's siblings. One had had glaucoma and had an eye removed at eleven months. Another had no stomach lining and had to be fed on a special diet. Two had died of cancer, as had Heidi herself by then, and so had the father. Now I was starting to have trouble with Teddy. It all started one Saturday morning when he suddenly yelped and nipped a child in my house. I couldn't believe it. He loved children, and as a young dog would let them climb on him to get on to the sofa. Within a matter of weeks he had for no apparent reason suddenly snapped several times and the bites became more serious each time. I didn't like the look in his eyes and was sure he was in pain. I just wanted to get to Devon and get him sorted out. On the day we moved he bit the friend who was helping Martin move us. As the chap was taking the kennel down I excused it as trauma. The vet had put him on a drug to reduce his libido and keep him quieter. This made him sleepy and his eyes looked worse than ever. He was always all right with Martin and me and with us appeared a happy dog, but we had to keep him away from everyone else and could not trust him at all.

Before moving I had booked to take both Berns to a West Country show. We arrived and I took Teddy into the ring where, as usual, he won. I put him on the bench with a big PLEASE DO NOT TOUCH notice. I then went off to show Bella in the junior class. We were in the ring when I was shouted for on the Tannoy. Teddy had gone berserk on the bench and pulled a whole row of cages over. Other dogs had become very frightened and noisy which was making him worse, and people were shouting for the vet to came and dart him. There was nothing for it; I had to walk into a row of snapping snarling Bernese, who did not know me, release Teddy and get him away before he did any more damage. I looked him in the eye, released him, and walked him out to the car. I was given permission to leave early, collected Bella, and went home. One cannot keep a potentially dangerous dog, especially in a parsonage. For his sake and mine, my beautiful dog, the only one I have ever qualified for Cruft's, would have to be put to sleep. Like all my dogs, he died in my arms and a post-mortem showed that he had a massive tumour on the brain. It never was his fault and he was in pain, but he loved me to the end.

The Border Collie was also a disaster. I wanted a house pet to be my constant companion and she wanted to round up sheep. I sold her to a farmer and learned later that she was an exceedingly clever worker. He had her trained and she won trials and was a happy dog. My beautiful Bella was on her own and I was anxious for her to have pups.

Three months after our arrival in Devon I returned to Yarmouth for Martins' wedding in Hemsby, the parish where Shelly's family lived. It was very good to have the opportunity to come back for a few days and meet up with people again. I didn't feel so far removed from everyone. As they could not afford a honeymoon, Martin and Shelly spent one night in a hotel and then came back to Devon with me for the rest of the time.

The wedding over and a pattern of work established in the parish (I was supposed to work the equivalent of two days a week plus Sunday duty), I could now plan what my future with the dogs was to be. At one show I had been to I was very impressed with a breed of dog which looked to me very like a smaller version of an Elk hound. It certainly had the curly tail carriage characteristic of all Spitz breeds. Several of these dogs had panniers and collecting boxes on their backs for Hearing Dogs for the Deaf People. In a flash I knew I wanted one and I would breed for the HDFDP. I talked to many breeders, saying I was in no hurry but would like to know when a good breeding bitch turned up. About two years later I received a phone call saying that a breeder had found what she felt would be the ideal pup for me. I went to see her and two weeks later went to pick her up. There were five bitches in the litter and one dog pup that had been the first to go. The breeder announced proudly that as soon as the dog went, my pup had become the dominant one in the litter. My heart sank, as I knew the father was a very dominant dog. The pup was very sweet and obviously very people friendly, but I knew I had to teach her to submit. That night I had a prayer group in my house and sat all night with my little pup now named Kyle (which I felt was suitably Norwegian) lying on her back on my lap in the position of submission. As soon as she was old enough I took her each week to training classes where I was constantly told off for being too soft with her. I was not. She was just her dad all over again, and, despite him being a champion, I later learned that he had to be kennelled on his own because he made life hell for any other dog that came near him. I tried showing Kyle and she was much admired, but her behaviour let her down every time. By this time my friend and churchwarden, who had just lost another challenging dog, took her on to live with her and we tried to get her in pup. She was not having any of it and no dog wanted to get near her. After driving down to Cornwall several times we gave up, and my friend had her spayed. This quietened her a bit and she did settle very well as she got older and lived to a good age and I know gave back a lot of the love Jean lavished on her. However, she was not one of my success stories.

I then tried puppy walking for Hearing dogs. It was enjoyable and I had some lovely puppies. The standard is very high and none made the grade for a variety of reasons. Only those who are physically and temperamentally excellent are accepted for training, and as most of the dogs are rescued the numbers are very small. They decided I lived too far away to continue. Some good did come out of the venture. With the aid of my vet and a few friends, I started a local branch H.D.F.D.P. that grew quickly and went very well, raising a great deal of money for the charity. To my knowledge it is still going well.

Meanwhile I had taken my beautiful Bella to a dog of my original breeding on the Isle of Wight. There was a champion dog that appeared both in Bella's pedigree and in the dogs which I knew had thrown puppies with one blue eye. It was well back in the pedigrees and I was prepared to take the risk, as everything else seemed good. She gave birth to seven beautiful pups and I determined to keep the pick of the litter and start showing again. At four weeks I found that two of the litter had a blue eye, one my pick of litter. I had to sell them very cheap and kept the second best pup. Yogi did me very well, getting best puppy in show at two championship shows. That year, because of the huge number of entries, the Cruft's committee decided there would be no more puppy classes. I knew Yogi didn't have the bone of his blue-eyed brother and sold him to the owner of an antique shop who wanted a dog who would be a quiet presence in the shop and protect her. He fulfilled all her wants and needs and had a wonderful life. I gave her all the wonderful write-ups he had had as a puppy and she was overjoyed. I do not believe any dog has been more loved.

Bella had meanwhile been mated to the dog of the year, an imported dog that later went on to win the progeny class, though she was only his third bitch. The puppies all had wonderful heads but carried far too much white. Three out of six pups had one blue eye and as the rogue dog was nowhere in the father's pedigree I had to face the fact that it was my Bella who was carrying the bad gene and had her spayed. I told myself firmly that my twenty-five years of breeding was now at an end. I would keep my beautiful Bella as a pet and would puppy walk.

The next year I broke my right wrist square dancing and three weeks later with my right arm in plaster fell over on the cliff while out with the dogs and broke the elbow of my left arm. This had to be set in an operation and I was hospitalised for a week and pretty helpless for some time after. A breeder who had bought a pup from me and was very enthusiastic about Berns asked me if I would go and stay with her for a week or two to convalesce and to whelp her lovely imported bitch as she did not feel confident to do it. I readily agreed. We had eight beautiful puppies and when I was offered first pick of the pups in gratitude I knew that my breeding days were going to start again! It is impossible to choose a pup at a few days old. They were all well marked as far as I could see, so I chose a little girl who had a few white hairs on the back of her neck as a distinguishing mark which would go as she got older. She appeared very well marked and was born third. I never choose pups that are the first or last born or born after a long time in the birth canal, as these, I believe, could develop physical defects. When I went to collect my little Sophie I found that all the pups had been tested for temperament, all had done well, and Sophie had done best of all. Bella seemed to take over the training of Sophie and they became a wonderful pair of dogs.

However, with the end of my puppy walking days, I still wanted a smaller dog to be with me all the time. One day I read that Border Collie Rescue had a four year old bitch that had been working for a farmer who was too mean to have her spayed, had drowned two litters of pups and had brought her to rescue as he now had a dog working for him. I took Bella and Sophie to meet her and all decided they belonged together. It was too perfect to last. Little Holly looked a bit too well covered for a working dog and I decided her food must be regulated. A week later I found I should be feeding her up. She was undoubtedly pregnant but I had no idea when to expect the patter of tiny paws. She had them in my wardrobe, placing them tidily in my shoes. She refused all offers of a whelping box or comfortable bed, preferring the wardrobe or behind my bed. One day two of the pups crawled under the bed while I was out and in her panic she had ripped my sheets and all the side of my bed. Poor little girl—she must have been terrified of the thought of having more pups taken away. She was a wonderful mother and all the pups went to good homes. I had her spayed and she became all that I wanted and was my constant companion, going visiting, to church and on holiday to Ireland with me where she lived in the car with the door open. Like most Border Collies she was always at heel and hated the lead. I had her for two wonderful years after which she was poisoned—how or when I shall never know. I was heartbroken.

I arranged for Sophie to be mated to a dog who was much the same breeding as Bella but sadly, a week before she was ready to go, the dog died. There was little time to arrange anything and I took her to one of Bella's sons. She had three pups, all of which went to farms. Farmers were finding more and more that Bernese were an ideal breed to have around lonely farmhouses. They lived happily with Collies and other working dogs and because of their size and boldness they were a great deterrent to intruders. They were also very good with stock and quickly learnt friend from foe. Markings and looks were largely irrelevant; health and temperament were of paramount importance. In all, Sophie had three litters and I think all but one of her pups went to farms.

A couple in the parish bred working Labradors. I very much admired their young black bitch, a very gentle "one man" sort of Labrador. She was to have a litter. One day I said to them that if ever they had a little black bitch that might be a bit small to work, I would be interested. A litter of twelve pups were born, six black and six yellow. The first day two black ones died and I thought my chances had probably gone. Five weeks later, after the morning service, I was told, "Your puppy will soon be able to come home, would you like to come and see her?" I went round to their house. The seven largest pups had been weaned, but the three smallest had been taken indoors with Mum, two yellow ones and my little black girl. She was small enough to lie in the palm of my hand but full of mischief and so like a smaller edition of her beautiful Mum, she was irresistible.

Bella and Sophie, having both experienced motherhood, started to squabble over her and I began to wonder whether I had made a big mistake bringing a pup into the family. My vet suggested there were only two solutions—get rid of the puppy I had or get another puppy so that they had one each. Looking at the paper one day I saw that someone in Exeter had a litter of nine chocolate Labrador bitches. They were very expensive but I was curious to see what a chocolate Labrador was like, so I arranged to go and see them. Nine little sausages were running about, each wearing a different coloured woolly collar. I knew that six of the pups had been booked but I asked the breeder not to tell me which. I wanted time to select the pup I wanted and, if she had already been booked, I would take it as a sign I was not meant to have one. If, however, she had not gone I would take it as a sign I was meant to have her. I took time to make my choice—the pup that was not too dominant but who came to me and was not shy or nervous. I knew little of the finer points of Chocolate Labradors but I finally made my choice. She was one of the three not yet booked. I would have her. It was one of the best decisions I ever made. Bella took her as her pup, allowing Sophie full maternal rights over little Kim. There was just eight months between the two Labradors and they grew up together, later sharing maternal duties when they in turn had pups. Molly, as we called her, has had six litters and reared thirty-four pups successfully. She has been a "Pat dog" in the hospital and a blood donor for two vets. She loves everyone and welcomes cats, dogs and children. As a guard dog she is useless, but my little black Kim loves me and protects me so Molly is allowed to put out the welcome mat and sit drooling over guests with big amber eyes. I now seemed to have the perfect foursome for many years. In the end poor Bella died at a fairly young age and I acquired a yellow lab pup, even having a litter from her. I never took to her as much as the others and when my time came to leave Devon and retire to a bungalow, I decided three dogs were enough and left her with a young couple. They fell in love with her and could offer her plenty of one-to-one attention which she craved.

27

NEW CHALLENGES

After driving through the night we arrived in Devon at breakfast time. The neighbours were very welcoming and I got the impression that the parsonage had been empty for so long that a two-headed monster would have been made welcome. For days, people not only brought me cups of tea, but meals, plants for the garden and a host of other goodies. On the second day a party had been arranged at the village hall in my honour. Ten minutes before I was due to leave a man arrived with the new television and video I had bought with part of my Yarmouth Golden Handshake. I explained to him that I could not stay as I was expected at the village hall. He obviously thought I was being most unreasonable and quoted me an astronomical figure to allow him to take them away and come again. I said I could give him ten minutes. Half an hour later the organist arrived to see what had happened to me. Now very close to tears I explained my dilemma. He charged in and ordered the poor electrician out of the house, and carted me off to the village hall where I had to explain what had happened. What a beginning! Could it get worse? It could!

After my few days allowed for settling in, the vicar came to see me. He wanted me to go with him on the first Sunday to all the churches of the benefice to be introduced. I obviously could not do much until the bishop had been to license me. He mentioned that there was a chapter meeting next day, which I probably would rather not attend. I could see he was dreading it and suggested we took the deanery head on. After the Eucharist, and over coffee, Derek introduced me to the Rural Dean, who greeted me coldly. I then had to sit and listen to the chapter clerk read that the Brethren had registered their disapproval over the fact that the Rev. Derek Newport had appointed a woman in charge of part of his benefice. He had registered their disapproval to the bishop, who had said he had agreed to the appointment, and could do nothing about it. After the business a very evangelical priest read a paper on the "Masculinity of God"! Several of the chapters, including the chapter clerk, rang me following the meeting assuring me that it was not their idea but the rest who had protested!

The Rural Dean retired as Rural Dean, and soon after from parish ministry altogether. (He was getting near retirement anyway.) Strangely, the bungalow he had bought for his retirement was in my village. He spent the last two years of his working life with the Missions to Seamen. I often ran into him walking our dogs and he was always friendly. I felt I had a lot to prove. I later discovered that Exeter Diocese was the only diocese in the whole country to vote against Women Deacons. The Guinea Pig was in the hot seat again.

Duly licensed by the Bishop of Plymouth in my main church, I quickly felt at home and was made welcome wherever I went. There was, however, a lot of division in the parish over petty things, which seemed to be mainly between the new wardens and the old wardens who had resigned but would not keep quiet. At the first P.C.C. which was held in the chapel of ease—I am not sure how some of them refrained from throwing things across the aisle, and I watched Derek the vicar going white with anger. After the meeting I suggested that in future they should meet in the parsonage, in the hope they would be more restrained in my house than they were in the house of God! They did this for some years, and with the passage of time, healing took place. I think they had had so many changes that everyone was very jumpy and insecure. Whether it was because I was a woman or not, I never met anything but kindness and consideration from any of the church people and made many very good friends.

There was an obvious need for a ministry to holiday makers and I held a family service in the chapel of ease during the summer months. In August it was packed out with the children sitting all over the floor, even up beside the altar. I always asked at the beginning whether there was a priest in the congregation and, if there was, asked him to give the absolution and bless us at the end. It was amazing how many incognito priests appeared and gave us absolution in shorts and T-shirt.

My grandchildren, who spent most of the holidays with me, always told everyone that Grandma had two and a half churches, which in a way was true. The original church had been from the twelfth century at South Huish. In the 19th century most of the village of South Huish had disappeared, whereas the neighbouring villages of Galmpton and Hope Cove were growing fast. Galmpton was growing as a farming community, whereas Hope Cove folk were nearly all fisher folk. The church at South Huish gradually fell into a very bad state of repair and the dwindling community could not afford to do the necessary repairs. In about 1840 Lord Devon offered a piece of land and encouraged the building of a church at Galmpton and Holy Trinity was built. This became the parish church of the area. The tiny chapel of ease at Hope Cove had been a village school, and still had the old school bell. It is now a tiny church, or chapel of ease and is dedicated like many fishermen's churches to St Clement. The old church at South Huish was allowed to fall into ruin until the Friends of Friendless Churches took on the preservation of the site and the service of Evensong was held in the ruins every first Sunday in August. About two years before my arrival in the area the Friends of Friendless Churches had built a new altar from the ruined stone. I asked if this altar had ever been consecrated, and on finding it had not, decided we should ask the new Bishop of Plymouth to come and consecrate the altar and celebrate Communion for us. It was the very first thing the new Bishop did after his consecration. It was a wonderful afternoon and the sun shone. All the churches of the deanery sent representatives and, after the service, we served cold drinks and folk picnicked in the ruins. After that we had a service of Holy Cmmunionon on the first Sunday in August every year and it became very popular, especially with the holidaymakers, some of whom come year after year. The rest of the year sheep are grazed in the church to keep the grass down. Driving past there one summer evening at dusk I saw a huge ram with very handsome horns standing in front of the altar and was reminded of the old pictures of the Lamb of God. For many it is a very special place.

28

MAKING ENDS MEET

Time went very quickly in Hope Cove and I kept very busy. The idea that retired folk doing a "House for duty" do Sunday duty and work two days a week in addition is ridiculous. Nobody works part-time for God. Also, I found it very difficult living without any sort of salary coming in. My church pension was calculated in such a way that it was only half what it would have been had I not married and had a large family. I tried doing nursing at nights but could not do the lifting so gave that up and went on a register of agency nurses which was much better but not so well paid. For eighteen months I slept three nights a week with an elderly confused lady as well as having to go out when called if free to do so. The variety was enjoyable but did not always mix too well with parish commitments.

Then I decided to enquire about fostering again and for twelve weeks drove every week into Plymouth to retrain. Most of the others were young or middle aged couples. I was definitely the Granny of the group, which was marked on the last night when I found the others had had a whip round and presented me with a beautiful pot plant. I was licensed to take two teenagers over thirteen and would be paid extra to take emergencies when I had a vacancy. To write of all the wonderful young people who came and stayed with me would make another book. I enjoyed them all, some for a few hours, some for years. No day was dull and somehow it fitted in so well with my church commitments. I wished I had done it from the beginning and I would recommend it to anyone living alone as I was.

One of the joys of living in South Devon in the summer is that folk do visit for a holiday and, in turn, all the family and many friends come. One great highlight was a visit from Ines and Dave from Ottawa. They first holidayed in Europe and then came on to me for their last fortnight. I think I saw more of Devon in that fortnight than at any other time, as I was able to drive them around, and they in turn treated me to meals out. Ines and I once again took on from where we had left off. She was already beginning to suffer with arthritis, so we took the days slowly and played cards and nattered in the evening. It all ended far too quickly and I have not seen them since.

These were turbulent times in the Church. I found being an ordained deacon, with pastoral care for my own churches and villages, hugely satisfying, and at no time did I feel called to the priesthood, although it was fairly obvious that most of the women deacons in the Diocese did. I loathed all of the "Women's" meetings but felt either I had to go or be seen as unfriendly. Most of them were a lot younger than I and I did feel for them although not sharing their passionate feelings. I continued my enormous interest in "Churches Together" and was very concerned about church unity. I read as much as I could and fully understood the predicament that Ronald Runcie, the then Archbishop of Canterbury, was in. He had spent a great deal of time cultivating good relations with the Roman Catholic Church and to ordain women in the Church of England would almost inevitably result in what he would see as a backward step. However, he also had the Worldwide Anglican Communion to consider and in many parts of the world the ministry of women had long been a *fait accompli*. Women priests from the States, from New Zealand, and other parts, were coming to England and could not celebrate the Eucharist in their own country or with their own friends. The media got in on the act in a big way and the future of Anglicanism was at stake. The next few General Synods were nightmares and I believe that many people, both clergy and laity, hoped that the vote should be put if only in the hope that it would be a "No" vote and all would go quiet for a few years. In the spring of 1992 a preliminary vote to test the feelings of the Church was put to the Spring Synod in York. It resulted in a two-thirds majority in the Houses of Bishops and Clergy but not in the House of Laity—far too close for anyone's comfort. The result was a summer of rallies, in which many M.Ps were asked to speak and nail their colours to the mast. Was this not the established church at stake! It was also election year and the Conservative Government had been returned with a majority which surprised even them. Were the ordinary people getting more and more afraid of change?

On November 11th 1992 the vote was finally put at Church House, and much to most people's surprise, was passed in all three houses. *Everyone* was surprised! Some wept, some rejoiced, congregations were split, clergy resigned and Ann Widdecombe was received into the Roman Catholic Church. I was shattered! I believe that all those who had been praying for many months for the right outcome were asking, "Lord, what are you doing to your church?"

29

TO BE OR NOT TO BE

My first reaction to the vote was to say "This is not for me." I felt I was too old; after all, I had been retired for seven years. As it happened I had a meeting with my Spiritual Director arranged for the morning of the "Vote" and I realised that for him a "yes" vote would, in his eyes, be the end of the Church of England. That same afternoon was the monthly service of Healing and Reconciliation in Galmpton. I felt I could not take this as "women" appeared to be causing so much suffering to the Church and I was carrying an unbearable burden of guilt on my "sisters'" behalf. I had already asked the vicar to take the service and to celebrate Communion for the healing of the Church, which he willingly did. I had videotaped the whole day's proceedings and sat up all night listening to the speeches and watching the faces and reactions as the vote was put.

I found it hard to take on the depths of feelings on both sides, both the victory celebrations on the one side and the absolute depths of despair on the other. Was it really about victory between warring factions, or was it, as I tended to believe, that the Church had prayed, listened and voted in a true attempt to know the mind of God and it was essential that we move forward into the unknown together.

While watching and listening to the speeches and the voting on television, I had seen a friend of mine in the House of Laity appear on camera and saw she looked ill with the strain. I knew she had for many years been canvassing against women's ordination and had voted against at the York Synod. I also knew that it required only three lay members to change their vote for the vote to go through, so closely was it in balance. I knew Angela to be a very committed woman of prayer, who tried in every way to be open to the promptings of the Holy Spirit and, when I rang her a week later and found she had been one of the three, because she had become more and more convinced that this was what God was asking of her although she had not made up her mind finally until the speeches ended, I knew I had to consider my position very carefully.

Several weeks later I received a communication from "Affirming Catholicism," including an address by the Dean of Exeter confessing to changing his views. He had decided to support women' priesting but was anxious within this to uphold the catholicity of the Church of England and was looking for the support of like-minded clergy. I gladly joined but felt I was moving slowly in a direction that had not until then existed. Was God asking me to be a guinea pig once again?

Strangely enough I found prayer very difficult at this time, partly, I think, because I was carrying a great burden of corporate guilt. This was something I found hit many of us who had been women workers in the church for many years, and did not seem to affect the younger women, or those newly trained. It took me a long time, and it was several years after my ordination to the priesthood, before I was to start to feel completely free of these feelings.

One good thing for those with doubts was that we all knew that, although the vote had been passed in Synod, it would be a long time before it went before Parliament. The first woman prime minister seemed to have little or nothing to say about the position of women in the Church and two of her ministers had a great deal to say against women becoming priests. For two and a half years we were left in limbo, which was very hard for those in training, as few appointments could be made.

In Exeter diocese the Bishop asked all women considering ordination to write to him as soon as possible and by a certain date. I was not considering it, so did not write. I did however go and see our Rural Dean who was a very good personal friend and I knew to be opposed in principle. We had a very good and open talk and I shared with him my feelings at the time. We agreed that all that mattered was that I, personally, was open to God's will to be done in me, even if that meant once again being a guinea pig. If it was God's will, neither he nor anyone else had a right to stop it. Finally I asked straight out, "If I am priested, will you use me in the deanery?" He replied, "I will use you wherever you will be welcome, and I think you should let the Bishop decide, but don't ask me to lay hands on you." He was as good as his word. On the evening before my ordination retreat he brought me a lovely card and flowers and prayed with me, but found an excuse not to be at the ordination.

I telephoned the Director of Ordinands, apologised for not replying to the bishop's letter, and asked if I was too late to be considered for the Petertide ordinations. We arranged for me to go and see the DOR in Exeter. He took down almost my whole life story and I emphasised my ill health and the fact that I was already 67 and was it worth it. I think, looking back, I was doing everything in my power to shift the responsibility onto anyone else. I was extremely mixed up.

I remember little of my interview with the bishop, which followed the following week, except that we had a long discussion on authority. We agreed that what had happened was not an issue of "women's rights" but about the "authority of the priesthood." He seemed to crystallise many of my doubts and fears and put into words feelings I had found hard to express. What I do remember most clearly was that at the end of the interview he came round from behind his desk, held my coat for me, and said, "You have a good understanding of authority, and because you aren't getting any younger I think it is essential that you are ordained priest at Petertide. However, it would help if you and a few others were ordained by the Bishop of Plymouth in St Mary's Plympton and not at the cathedral." I assured him I would prefer this. Little did I want to face all the razzmatazz of the cathedral with M.O.W. out in force and the demonstrations of the opposition.

I drove home in a daze, aware of what was happening to me and feeling as I had before my first operation that fate or God was dictating my life in an extraordinary way and all decision-making had been taken out of my hands, as I must have known it ultimately would be. I imagine it is how a condemned man or a terminally ill person feels.

There was one more thing I had to do. I had to experience a woman celebrating and know whether I would know the "Real Presence" as really as in those early days in the convent when I had met Our Lord in the Blessed Sacrament. The Canterbury ordinations were in March, and I had received a prayer card from a very old college friend. I decided to go to her first mass. It was a long journey from Plymouth to Canterbury. I booked in at a guesthouse near the church and wandered around Canterbury until shortly before the service. I was still not sure whether I would receive communion when the time came, but the delight on Pamela's face when she saw me made it all worth while and I was glad I had taken my camera. When the time of the consecration arrived I had no doubts whatsoever and Jesus came to me in a very real and precious way. How I wish some of those who are still having so much difficulty would do what I did and let Jesus speak to them.

A couple of weeks later I would once again be at High Leigh. I decided to wait until then before sending my final letter to the bishop and accepting my place at the Plymouth Ordination. I had not been feeling very well, experiencing a lot of chest pain, no doubt due to all the extra emotional stress; so on the second evening I decided to go and ask for anointing and to go to a Priest who did not know me and would not be aware of my trauma. I am not sure that he even knew

I was a deacon. My churchwarden and very good friend was with me. Fr David anointed me with the oil of healing and the team prayed for me. Then Fr David said, "And now for anointing for your ministry." He picked up the chrism oil and as soon as he touched me I was a heap on the floor where I remained for the next half-hour. I was aware of much going on around me, but I was wisely left in peace. My main thought during this time was of the disciples in the upper room being breathed upon and I knew that Pentecost would surely have to follow. There was no turning back. God would give his Guinea Pig all that was necessary to do what was demanded of her as He had done so many times in the past.

Through all this Derek, my vicar, was wonderful. I knew how much he wanted me to be priested and how much it would help the benefice to have another priest, but never at any stage did he put any pressure on me. He remained sensitive to my turmoil and was always there for me when I needed him. I also knew he was in turmoil himself as he was contemplating a move. If he were to change parishes it would have to be done before he was much older. There was no doubt that my priesting would make things a lot easier for him and for the parishes. As soon as I returned from High Leigh I told him it was full steam ahead. He was overjoyed.

It was presumed, at first, that all the women would have their retreat at the Anglican Convent in Plymouth. As it turned out, there were too many of us and the nuns were not at all sure that they wanted us. However, the monks at Buckfast Abbey in Newton Abbot were delighted to have ladies in their guesthouse, and made us most welcome. Every evening we said compline with them in the abbey, and fraternised over meals. On the second day a noisy and excitable party of the League of Catholic Mothers arrived for a day conference. We knew they were bursting to talk to us, and I found I knew some of them, but we refused to let them break our silence.

For the eight of us who were to be ordained at Plympton the "Retreat" began with a rehearsal and tea party in the church. There were six deacons to be ordained priest and two young men who were to be ordained deacon. Compared with the cathedral it was to be a low-key affair. After tea the five women deacons departed to meet the rest at Buckfast. There were to be three parallel ordinations that day in the diocese, each to be presided over by one of the three Bishops. The Bishop of Exeter would preside at the Cathedral, the Bishop of Plymouth at Plympton, and the Bishop of Crediton at Crediton church for all the men who refused to be ordained with us. However, the Bishop of Crediton took our retreat and confessed to us he had been ordaining women for years in America and was a great friend of Barbara Harris, the first woman Anglican bishop on whom he had laid hands at her consecration. The Diocesan Bishop was anxious that all three bishops of the diocese would be equally "tainted" by having laid hands on women. However, the Archdeacon of Exeter was later consecrated as the first "Flying Bishop" (Bishop with alternative episcopal oversight).

On June 26th, 1994, the Guinea Pig became a priest. I have no idea how many laid hands on me. All I know is that I had an overwhelming feeling that history was being made, and I had done the right thing.

30

MANY GUINEA PIGS

My first celebration of communion was to be on Tuesday evening in the parish church of Malborough. Although I was convinced by now that it was right for me to be a priest, I was still very aware of the disunity and hurt which was being caused by what I had done. I had written my own service based on the Rite A Service for Church Unity in the Alternative Service book. All the hymns, prefaces etc. were for Unity.

The chairman of High Leigh, Father James Naters, came and preached for me; my sons and grandchildren served me, and many priest friends stood round me and concelebrated. (Nine Priests in all.) I could not have been more loved and supported. Even several of my shell-shocked Catholic friends were in the congregation. As a parishioner said to me next morning, "The power of the Holy Spirit could be felt very strongly throughout the service."

I am writing this some eight years after those first ordinations in 1994, and things have moved on apace. Many women now have quite a high profile in the church, many are rural deans and several are archdeacons. Soon, no doubt, there will be bishops. There are still those who remain outside and have put themselves under Alternative Episcopal Oversight. It is still quite a mess. However, I believe, like many other things, it is God's mess and we are all in a learning process. There is no doubt that those of us who were ordained in '94 were the guinea pigs and were under the spotlight. In those early days I was in a holiday area and was very anxious that holiday-makers should not be caught out by coming to Church and be embarrassed by finding a woman celebrant. I asked the vicar if we could put on the list of services outside the church who was taking the service. He refused, and I later had to admit he was right. Time and time again, as I stood at the back of the church after Sunday morning worship, people would come up to me and say something like, "When I saw you were a woman I felt uncomfortable (or nervous or frightened) but I enjoyed the service and next time I won't feel so bad." Others would go to great lengths to tell me they had a WOMAN in their parish.

I still felt it was against Christian charity to catch people out and always made a point of going out before the service and kneeling at the altar rail so that if anyone wished to, they could leave without my being aware of it. Quite often people stayed but did not make their communion, and I understood, and made a point of talking to them over coffee after the service. I am aware that I was extremely lucky in the acceptance I received and that many others had a very hard time in their parishes and in Chapter. However, the relationship between any parish priest and his or her people is a very precious, difficult and often very emotive thing and, to my mind, the gender of the priest is of very secondary importance.

In a way I was thrown in the deep end because, shortly after my ordination, Derek announced that he was leaving for pastures new and we were to have an interregnum. There were four churches in the benefice. The other retired priest was to look after the two northern parishes and I would look after my patch and the Parish Church of Malborough. With the wardens' permission I made an office for myself in the study of the empty vicarage which housed the photocopiers and printer, and did my best to keep everything going as it always had. We all worked hard together; we kept numbers up, and I think everything ran very smoothly for the next year. Towards the end there was also a vacancy in Salcombe, so it quite frequently meant four services a Sunday as well as several midweek ones as well. I also continued to try and keep up Derek's contact with our local village school and his rota of fortnightly communions for the housebound. That year it was our church's turn to host the confirmation and we did not want to let the deanery down. I had seven children and two adults receiving instruction and that summer we hosted a confirmation for about thirty folk of all ages. I enjoyed every minute of it, but, as I still had two foster children at home and others that visited frequently for a chat, I did get quite exhausted.

In addition to all this I did have to think what I was going to do as soon as an appointment was made. I had no home and I was nearly seventy. I knew that the pensions board would buy me a house in one of the three dioceses in which I had worked, but not in London or Southwark. I loved Exeter and, at first, was strongly tempted to go to North Devon, but decided that, as I got older, it would be too far away from the family. Really, the choice was between Portsmouth where Clare still lived or to go back to Norwich. I decided on the latter and wrote to Bishop Peter Nott to ask him if he would have me back as a priest with permission to officiate. He replied that he would gladly have me back but not in Great Yarmouth. I had no desire, after nine years of rural ministry, to go back into town; but as Martin and Shelly live in the north part of Yarmouth, I decided to look somewhere in the Fleggs for a bungalow of which the Pensions Board would approve. I gave myself four days to come up and find somewhere, and after a frantic house hunt submitted to the board for their approval, in order of preference, a cottage and three bungalows. I was given my first preference and count myself very blessed.

Meanwhile, an appointment was made and an excellent parish priest with a delightful young wife was chosen unanimously by the whole benefice. Sadly, it was not a freehold and he was appointed as priest in charge for five years, and all were to continue to live under the ongoing threat of more parish reorganisation. The induction was to take place at the beginning of September and I agreed that I would leave three weeks later.

It must have been very hard for John Sweetman, and I shall always be grateful to him for his forbearance and tact as he allowed the Mothers' Union, the school, the Sunday School, the Council of Churches, and many other groups to say goodbye to me, waiting for another meeting to be welcomed himself. He spent the first three weeks in my shadow and I felt for him, but could not do anything about it. I am quite sure he was pleased to see the back of me although he would never admit it and went out of his way to help in giving me a wonderful send off. I knew the benefice would, at least for the next five years, be in the hands of a truly Christian Pastor. My last service was to be a Songs of Praise one Sunday evening. I made it into a kind of Desert Island Discs, choosing hymns to illustrate my life story from the war years to my ordination. The church was packed and there were even holidaymakers who had come from Dorset for the evening. I received so many gifts and my "Golden Handshake" was unbelievable.

On October 1st 1996 I arrived at Barton Way in Orrmesby St Margaret to my new life in retirement. Two evenings later I walked the dogs to the fields at the end of the road. It was a glorious October evening; the sunset was magnificent as it glinted on a patchwork of crops of various colours. On the horizon the wind pylons at West Somerton swirled in the evening breeze. The flat East Anglian landscape, so different from the Devon hills, made it appear to me as a Dutch painting, and I felt completely at peace. I had definitely done the right thing.

It was very hard at first, and I know I upset a lot of people. After just one year of being the nearest I shall ever be to being a parish priest, and quite a popular one full of good ideas, I suddenly had to realise that no one was interested in my ideas anymore, and for the first time in my working life I had no responsibility. I was expected to fill in gaps for the local clergy, to be useful when required, and to keep quiet. It proved a great lesson in loyalty and humility. I threw myself into charity work and started breeding cats, which ran me into debt. It is hard for a mentally active person to stop. Community service lads came and laid out my garden for me and I acquired a few chickens. I loved my bungalow and gradually started to get things as I wanted them and to learn to enjoy life alone. After a year of struggle I really did start to count my blessings once again.

EPILOGUE

I have now been retired seven years. My heart is slowly deteriorating and I have glaucoma and arthritis. I no longer drive a car and I go round the village in a mobility scooter. I have a comfortable bungalow, maintained by the Pensions Board, and a lovely garden. I also have Molly and Kim, my two faithful Labradors, who are growing old with me, four cats, four ducks and thirteen hens and just about enough money for us all to live on. Above all, I have a wonderful family that I try not to burden too much, many very good friends and have been given the gift of a computer to keep my brain challenged. God is being very gracious to his Guinea Pig and she is ready to meet Him when He calls. In the meantime I pray that He may continue to use me in whatever way He wishes. I am very content!

About the Author

Reverend Margaret Anne Freeman was born in 1927 with a serious and complicated heart defect, Fallot's Tetralogy. She was not expected to live very long at all, let alone walk or have children. She defied expectations, and today works as a 76 year old retired priest in Norfolk. Her autobiography tells how she gained and kept her Christian faith during war and countless personal tragedies, whilst breaking records as she went. She became the first adult to survive open-heart surgery, and the first such survivor to have children. It also tells of the enormous struggle she had over the Ordination of women in the Church of England.

0-595-31056-7

Printed in the United Kingdom
by Lightning Source UK Ltd.
100277UKS00001BC/7